**Chicago Tribune**

# SUPER BEARS

THE REMARKABL~~E~~ ~~STORY OF THE 200~~6 CHICAGO BEARS

# Chicago Tribune

**PUBLISHER** Scott C. Smith
**EDITOR** Ann Marie Lipinski
**MANAGING EDITOR, NEWS** George de Lama
**MANAGING EDITOR, FEATURES** James Warren

# SUPER BEARS

## THE REMARKABLE STORY OF THE 2006 CHICAGO BEARS

**SPORTS EDITORS** Dan McGrath, Michael Kellams

**PHOTO EDITORS** Torry Bruno, Todd Panagopoulos, Robin Daughtridge, Keith Swinden

**WRITERS** John Kass, Rick Morrissey, Mike Downey, Don Pierson, David Haugh, John Mullin, Melissa Isaacson, Fred Mitchell, Dan McGrath

**COPY EDITORS** Tom Carkeek, Mike Sansone, Jim Harding

**ART DIRECTORS** Joan Cairney, Chuck Burke

**GRAPHICS EDITOR** Steve Layton

**IMAGING** Don Bierman, Christine Bruno, Kathy Celer

**PROJECT MANAGERS** Bill Parker, Susan Zukrow

**Triumph Books**
542 S. Dearborn St. Suite 750
Chicago, IL 60605
Phone: (312) 939-3330
Fax: (312) 663-3557
Printed in
the United States of America
ISBN: 978-1-60078-032-5

**COVER PHOTO** John Smierciak
**BACK COVER** Heather Stone

**FLAG DAY:** Punter Brad Maynard leads the Bears onto the field at Dolphin Stadium for the Super Bowl.
NUCCIO DI NUZZO

**BROTHERS IN ARMS:** Defensive standouts Lance Briggs (55), Tank Johnson and Brian Urlacher prepare to go to work in Miami. JIM PRISCHING

*By* JOHN KASS

# Sting makes Chicago reel

IN THE SUPER BOWL WEEK of 60 million words leading up to just 60 minutes of football, you were bound to hear somebody say something crazy. But I didn't think it would be the cautious, soft-spoken, gentlemanly Tony Dungy, coach of the Super Bowl champion Indianapolis Colts.

"We're not a city that's won a lot of championships. We're not like Chicago," Dungy said a few days before his team whipped our underdog Bears in Super Bowl XLI, which is Latin for 29-17. "It would be great for our city for that reason."

Chicago? A city of champions? Jeepers.

It sounded sincere, and coming from Dungy there is little doubt it was sincere. But still a bit odd, as every sports fan in Chicago would testify if we were ever called before a grand jury.

If Dungy said, "We're not a city that has a lot of political corruption, we're not like Chicago," we'd believe him. Indianapolis isn't even an expansion team in the Indictment League. Chicago pols have led us to victory in so many Federal Mail Fraud Statute Bowls that we've stopped counting.

So we're perennial champions in something, at least. But Chicago as a city that has won a lot of sports championships? Chicago?

No, and that's the sting of it.

Except for the White Sox winning the World Series in 2005, the Sox and the hapless Cubs have combined to go almost two centuries without a trophy. That comes to about two centuries of civic hope in the spring, followed by two centuries of sipping the bitter dregs in the fall. Somebody will mention the Bulls, and yes, the Michael Jordan Bulls won six world championships. But the problem is that they merely played basketball, which, like hockey, almost counts but doesn't, really.

The fact is that when it comes to Chicago's heart, there is only one tie that binds. The Bears. And they gave us a heck of a season. They got to the final game. They didn't win it. But they got there—and took us with them.

Chicago is a great sports town, but Bears football is what joins all the divided houses, including mine, and perhaps yours too. Those Cubs fans among us, and Sox fans as well, keep bickering. Two centuries of mostly futility will do that to the mind.

We're a region of tribes, by politics and ethnicity, by income and by belief. But for all our differences, the Chicago Bears have been our common ground.

"We just remember this feeling," linebacker Lance Briggs said, "and let it sting until we get back here."

The week leading up to the Super Bowl was all about hype and words that didn't mean much, words like "deserve," which has little to do with sports in Chicago.

But Lance Briggs talked about letting it sting. That's something every Chicago fan understands.

**THE PARTY'S OVER:** Devin Hester absorbs a disappointing scene as confetti flies after the Colts' Super Bowl victory. SCOTT STRAZZANTE

# CONTENTS

**HAPPY TO BE HERE:** Wide receiver Bernard Berrian wears a huge smile as he charges onto the field before the game. Berrian caught four passes for 38 yards.

SCOTT STRAZZANTE

*By* RICK MORRISSEY

# Next year? Join the club

THE WHOLE IDEA was a championship season. It was a grand idea. A big idea. Make no small plans and all that.

From Day One of training camp, the Bears talked about winning the Super Bowl. They had every right. They came into the 2006 season with the best defense in football. They were that good.

They came up short. A 29-17 loss to the Indianapolis Colts in Super Bowl XLI took care of those grand plans, but it couldn't make a very good season inconsequential.

The first five weeks of the season were a revelation. The defense, as expected, was dominant. Rex Grossman looked like everything the Bears had insisted he was. They seemed to have a real live quarterback for the first time in eons.

But the comeback victory against the Cardinals on a Monday night—as breathtaking as it was, as wonderful as Devin Hester was—exposed some very deep cracks in the Bears' foundation. Grossman threw four interceptions that night.

One of the truths of this season is that Grossman would have been much better off playing with a good team or an average team instead of a very good team. His mistakes wouldn't have been scrutinized so closely.

Chicago thought it had another Super Bowl champion on its hands. It didn't need a kid quarterback putting that dream in peril. When Good Rex was good, the city seemed to breathe easier. When Bad Rex showed up, people called talk shows and vented. They needed Dr. Phil.

There were big highlights for this team. Thomas Jones rushed for 1,210 yards. Brian Urlacher was Brian Urlacher. Hester was jaw-dropping. Bernard Berrian became the No. 1 receiver. Eight Bears made the Pro Bowl.

But there were problems too. Defensive tackle Tank Johnson had his well-chronicled troubles with the law, and the Bears decided to keep him on the roster even though he blatantly ignored their demands that he clean up his life.

Injuries to safety Mike Brown and defensive tackle Tommie Harris were huge. So, in a way, despite their stellar record, the Bears were almost as up-and-down as Grossman was.

But they carried on, all the way to the Super Bowl. There's something almost noble in that, in the idea of a team being greater than the sum of its parts.

But they wanted more. That was the whole idea.

Now Chicago is left with a concept it knows only too well: next year.

**MOST VALUABLE PEYTON:** Behind protection from his line, Super Bowl MVP Peyton Manning gets off a quick throw in the third quarter. SCOTT STRAZZANTE

*By* MIKE DOWNEY

# Empty, not empty-handed

SOMEBODY HAS TO LOSE A SUPER BOWL, and somebody did. It turned out to be the Bears, but not before they recaptured their stature as a mighty superpower of professional football and as the one team, baseball being a North-South civil war, that each side of Chicago adores.

By season's end, the Bears once again were princes of the city.

A dinosaur skeleton at a museum was attired in the team's urban outfit.

A cap sat jauntily atop Mr. Picasso's sculpture.

A couple of stone lions at the Art Institute wore supersized helmets, a reminder to all who passed by that a Super Bowl beast was back in town and on the prowl.

The Indianapolis Colts ultimately got in the last lick, winning the Super Bowl 29-17.

Not even tens of thousands of Bears fans in the stands could overcome the passing skills of Peyton Manning, easily the most dazzling artist on the Miami field, unless you care to count the one occasionally known as Prince.

Might the outcome have been different had outstanding defensive tackle Tommie Harris not been hurt in Game 12 and incapacitated thereafter? Well, maybe. He took on opponents two at a time, this kid did, and the Bears' proud defense was not the same without him. Harris would have been a real handful for the Colts.

And what about safety Mike Brown, down since midway through the season with a foot injury

Never forget, however, that 32 teams fight it out in the National Football League, and 31 go home empty-handed.

Also do not minimize a nice piece of hardware that did end up in the Bears' hands. That would be the George S. Halas Trophy, which goes to the NFC champion. Rest assured that Virginia McCaskey would never consider that going home empty-handed.

It might be years—decades, even—before the Bears get this close again to a larger, even more priceless trophy.

Or perhaps it will be fairly soon that they get to finish what they have started. They could go to Glendale, Ariz., you know, to try their luck again in Super Bowl XLII because, keep on reminding yourself, somebody has to go to that game and win it.

Might as well be the Bears. Their city loves to see them succeed, almost as much as it loves seeing Bears apparel being worn by the neighborhood dinosaurs and lions.

**CHICAGO'S HOPE: Despite very high highs and very low lows, Rex Grossman has the backing of his teammates.** JIM PRISCHING

*By* DAVID HAUGH

# Earning an 'A' in chemistry

BEFORE THE FIRST PLAYOFF GAME against the Seattle Seahawks, cornerback Charles Tillman tried illustrating what made this season special for the Bears. Tillman asked an interviewer to close his eyes while the cornerback rubbed his arm.

"What am I doing?" Tillman asked.

"Rubbing my arm."

"How do you know?"

"I feel it."

"Exactly."

Exactly, indeed.

It's hard to describe what made the Bears emerge as the best team in the NFC in 2006. But after an amazing opening stretch of the season punctuated by a comeback from a 20-point deficit at Arizona without an offensive touchdown, it just felt like the Bears' year.

Unlike the 1985 Bears, the 2006 version melded a chemistry that carried them to the Super Bowl mostly behind closed doors. As Rex Grossman said during Super Bowl week when asked about comparisons to the '85 Bears, this team had charisma, too, but simply didn't make a video to show the world.

But the indelible image of Lovie Smith's Bears will not be of Devin Hester's 108-yard return of a missed field against the Giants or anything Grossman or Thomas Jones or Bernard Berrian did on the field. It came in the locker room of University of Phoenix Stadium after the improbable win over the Cardinals. The Bears celebrated like a bunch of guys who truly were happy for each other as much as each was for himself.

They needed those bonds of brotherhood to help them endure the unusual amount of controversy that dogged a 13-3 team good enough to repeat as NFC North champion. There was the attention paid the unpredictable comments of Cedric Benson, the one-game suspension of Ricky Manning Jr. after he pleaded no-contest to an assault last April, the fallout from Tank Johnson's arrest and the shooting incident that killed his best friend. But the most constant rallying point for the Bears was Grossman, whose season will be remembered as one of the most scrutinized in Chicago sports history.

That will continue into next season after a 29-17 Super Bowl loss to the Indianapolis Colts in which Kelvin Hayden returned a Grossman interception 56 yards for a touchdown on the game's pivotal play. But in defeat, as in victory, the support from teammates never wavered.

"Rex brought us the Super Bowl," Alex Brown said. "The Super Bowl hadn't been to Chicago in 21 years. They should give him a break. We're upset, but we won the NFC championship with Rex."

Many Bears vowed to return to the stage they stumbled on in Miami. But as players slowly filed out of the locker room after losing to the Colts, just as many were too busy looking back to start looking ahead. A year that felt so right had ended so wrong.

"When you say 'Super Bowl or bust,' it takes a little bit out not to finish it," Lance Briggs said. "The season still is what it was."

What it was, more than anything, was unforgettable.

**CAN'T PESTER HESTER:** Colts kicker Adam Vinatieri stretches vainly in an attempt to stop Devin Hester on his game-opening kickoff return. SCOTT STRAZZANTE

*By* DON PIERSON

# Hungry for another run

BEARS FANS WON SUPER BOWL XLI going away. In noise and numbers, they overwhelmed Colts fans in Miami, reminding both teams of Chicago's rich legacy. Clearly, Chicagoans were not prepared to lose. More is expected—and soon. The Bears win NFL championships about every two decades: 1985, 1963, 1946. So they are overdue. If they don't win next year, it will mark the longest title drought ever for a franchise that counts nine world championships and more Hall of Fame players than any other city.

Their fans outnumbered Colts fans everywhere you looked in Miami. One foursome entered the stadium wearing the jerseys of Payton, Sayers, Butkus and Urlacher.

You would have thought that would have been enough.

Devin Hester became the first to return an opening Super Bowl kickoff for a touchdown, and the immediate chorus of "Bear Down, Chicago Bears" never sounded better or louder.

But the Bears were unable to reach their season-long goal: to finish.

Teams that lose Super Bowls often go into hibernation.

Five of the last six Super Bowl losers have failed to make the playoffs the next season. But the Bears remain a young team with an old tradition.

This disappointment will only whet the appetite for next season and subsequent seasons.

Back-to-back playoff teams for coach Lovie Smith have restored an excitement missing since Da Coach, Mike Ditka, dominated the 1980s despite winning only one Super Bowl.

This team reached the playoffs last season and now the Super Bowl, so Smith's battle cry for 2007 becomes obvious.

After the White Sox won the World Se-

ries in 2005, Brian Urlacher said the celebration made him jealous.

The six NBA titles won by the Bulls in the 1990s set a standard for sports excellence not seen in Chicago since the Bears were the Monsters of the Midway with their four titles in the 1940s.

Getting close is more frustrating than satisfying for the Bears and their fans these days.

Expectations will only get bigger. With the new Soldier Field providing the revenue to compete in the free-agent market and the steady progress of team President Ted Phillips, general manager Jerry Angelo and Smith, the Bears have become a team equipped to earn greater expectations.

They had not lost an NFL title game since 1956, half a century ago. But this was only their third title appearance in that time.

The next half-century promises more. Losing is never the idea, but at least the Bears of 2006 proved getting there can be half the fun.

**GOT THEIR BACKS**: The Bears drew levels of strength from Brian Urlacher, who led the team in tackles. SCOTT STRAZZANTE

**LOOK OF LOVIE:** Scanning the field, coach Lovie Smith commands sideline attention. JOHN SMIERCIAK

# 13-3

The stoic **Lovie Smith.** The mercurial **Rex Grossman.** The electrifying **Devin Hester.** The metronomic **Robbie Gould.** The indomitable **Brian Urlacher.** They led a Bears team that went 13-3, won two NFC playoff games and earned a trip to Miami. Here's how they did it.

| FIRST QUARTER | SECOND QUARTER | THIRD QUARTER | FOURTH QUARTER |
|---|---|---|---|
| **26-0**<br>SEPT. 10 AT GREEN BAY | **40-7**<br>OCT. 8 VS. BUFFALO | **38-20**<br>NOV. 12 AT NEW YORK GIANTS | **42-27**<br>DEC. 11 AT ST. LOUIS |
| **34-7**<br>SEPT. 17 VS. DETROIT | **24-23**<br>OCT. 16 AT ARIZONA | **10-0**<br>NOV. 19 AT NEW YORK JETS | **34-31**<br>DEC. 17 VS. TAMPA BAY |
| **19-16**<br>SEPT. 24 AT MINNESOTA | **41-10**<br>OCT. 29 VS. SAN FRANCISCO | **17-13**<br>NOV. 26 AT NEW ENGLAND | **26-21**<br>DEC. 24 AT DETROIT |
| **37-6**<br>OCT. 1 VS. SEATTLE | **31-13**<br>NOV. 5 VS. MIAMI | **23-13**<br>DEC. 3 VS. MINNESOTA | **26-7**<br>DEC. 31 VS. GREEN BAY |

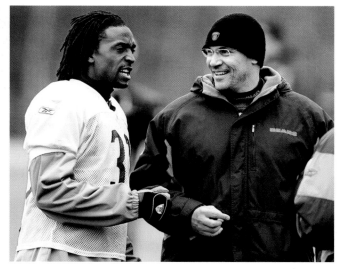

**DEFENSIVE DEMONS:** Cornerback Charles Tillman chats up coordinator Ron Rivera during practice. JIM PRISCHING

**WORTH A SHOUT-OUT:** Rashied Davis emerged as a go-to receiver, catching 22 passes and scoring twice. JOHN SMIERCIAK

# FIRST QUARTER

## GAMES 1-4

PACKERS  LIONS  VIKINGS  SEAHAWKS

# REX GROSSMAN

## Competitive fire drives quarterback; Urlacher's verdict: 'The kid's a winner'

REX GROSSMAN'S cousin Ben Cole still loves telling the story. When Grossman was in high school, he and Cole and another friend teamed to play in a popular three-on-three basketball tournament in Indianapolis, about 45 miles north of Grossman's hometown of Bloomington.

The morning of the tournament, Cole and his friend overslept after a night of partying. Grossman showed up on time, but by himself. Instead of forfeiting, Grossman took on the other three-man team alone ... and lost by a point.

"There's no better example than that to show what a competitor Rex is," Cole said.

The 2006 NFL season sure came close.

Entering the season, conventional wisdom suggested that it would be a good season for Grossman if he could stay healthy for 16 games. Two straight season-ending leg injuries had cast doubt on his durability. But after he played well enough in the first five games to generate talk of him being the league's MVP, the standards rose. So did the expectations.

What followed, as Grossman lapsed into inconsistency that included five games in which his passer rating sank lower than 40.0, was a season that exposed him to arguably as much scrutiny as any athlete in Chicago history. Grossman's mood was monitored closely by fans and media each week, and his psyche was read more voraciously than local newspapers.

When he took the podium after leading the Bears to the Super Bowl, as he had promised the day he was drafted in 2003, Grossman resisted the urge to say the four

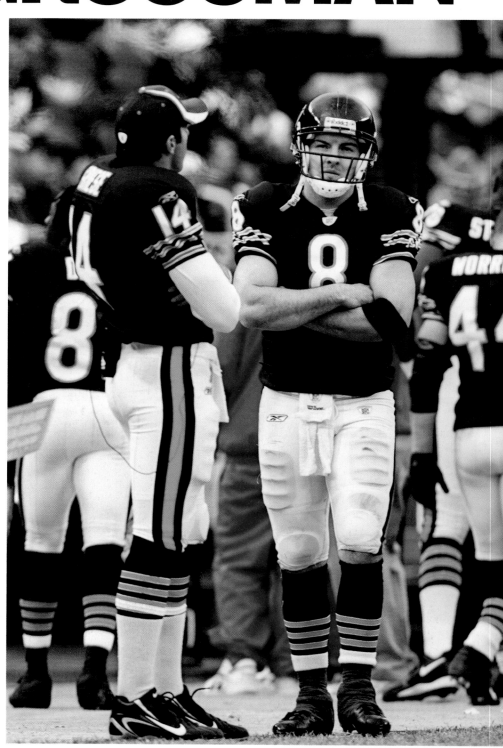

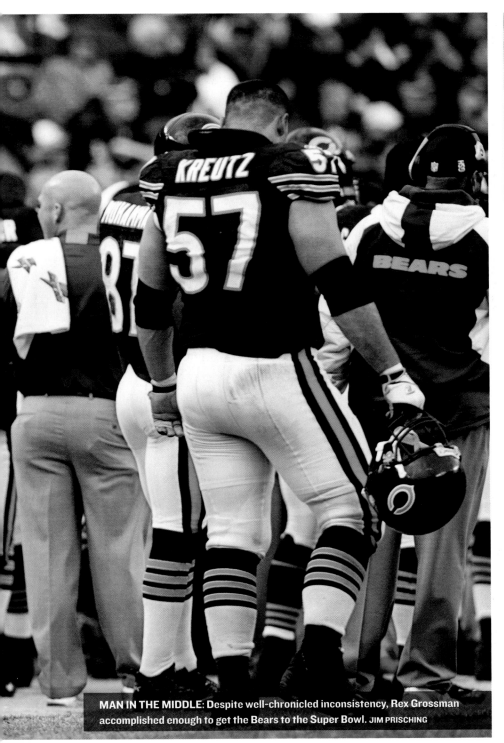

**MAN IN THE MIDDLE:** Despite well-chronicled inconsistency, Rex Grossman accomplished enough to get the Bears to the Super Bowl. JIM PRISCHING

**BOSOM BUDDIES:** Bernard Berrian chest-bumps Rex Grossman after the two hooked up for a 49-yard touchdown against the Packers. JIM PRISCHING

words that stayed on the tip of his tongue.

I.

Told.

You.

So.

"I mean, it doesn't get any better than this right now," Grossman said, wearing a smile and an "NFC Champions" hat after beating the Saints. "Redemption and all that, I mean, that's for you guys to write about."

The redemptive nature of Grossman's season dominated Super Bowl hype and overshadowed the biggest reality for the Bears about the 2006 season: They'd finally found their franchise quarterback.

Only one quarterback in Bears history, Erik Kramer, threw for more yards than Grossman. Grossman finished seventh in the league with 23 touchdown passes, 12th with 3,193 passing yards and second with seven games with a passer rating over 100. His serviceable overall passer rating of 73.9 in 2006 needs to improve if he is to take the next step into the elite echelon of NFL quarterbacks, but it mirrors that of other great quarterbacks such as Drew Brees and Brett Favre in their first full years as starters.

Grossman is far from a finished product. He locks in on his receivers too long at times, throws off his back foot rather than stepping into passes and looks to have lost some mobility after his leg injuries.

But as Grossman did in completing just 11 passes for 144 yards in the NFC championship game, as he did that one day on the basketball court in Indianapolis as a high school kid, he finds a way. He makes the best of what he has. And he competes.

"The kid's a winner," Brian Urlacher said.

Indeed, Grossman's 17-6 regular-season record as a starter makes him the winningest Bears starter dating back to 1961. It's that moxie that first put Grossman high on the Bears' draft board and what kept him sane during a season of wild emotional swings. It's also the trait that helped him endure season-ending injuries in 2004 and '05, when the only thing driving him during rehabilitation was the chance to lead the Bears where he led them this season.

Because as much as the debate raged over Good Rex and Bad Rex, it was always better for the Bears than No Rex, which is what limited them the last two seasons.

"You know, last couple years we knew we had a great team," Grossman said. "You look at our roster. Brian Urlacher, one of the best linebackers to ever play the game. Great offensive line. Alex Brown ... we have so many good guys ... Tommie Harris, Mike Brown, all these guys. You know you have a special team, and that's what makes you work that much harder in the off-season to get back healthy or to get stronger."

The strength Grossman developed this season had more to do with his mind than his body.

— *David Haugh*

**GOOD-HANDS GUY:** Desmond Clark added a new dimension as a pass-catching tight end.
SCOTT STRAZZANTE

**CRITIC'S CHOICE:**
While dodging tacklers and
barbs, Grossman managed to
throw for 3,193 yards.
HEATHER STONE

**SMALL TIPPER:** A Grossman pass barely eludes the gloved fingers of wide receiver Justin Gage. CHARLES CHERNEY

**FIVE BARS:** Or perhaps more for these very expressive Bears fans. HEATHER STONE

# REX SPANKS 'EM, 'D' BLANKS 'EM

## A first: Favre on wrong end of shutout

IF REX GROSSMAN was determined to put his shaky preseason performances behind him, he succeeded admirably, though temporarily. "Good Rex" had seldom been better. He completed 18 of 26 passes for 262 yards and a touchdown, a first-quarter 49-yard strike to Bernard Berrian that served notice that these Bears were willing and able to take chances down the field.

They also fulfilled a promise to rediscover their tight end as five of Grossman's completions went to Desmond Clark. Thomas Jones solidified his status as the Bears' best running back by rushing for 63 yards and protecting Grossman with strong blocking. Robbie Gould was perfect on four field-goal tries.

But in the end it was a day for defense. Brian Urlacher and company shut out Brett Favre and the Packers for the first time in 233 games. The Bears were so dominant that Green Bay ran just 20 plays from scrimmage in the first half. Favre, shut out for the first time in his career, looked every day of his 36 years and 11 months as the frisky Bears intercepted him twice and sacked him three times in their most one-sided trouncing of the Packers since a 61-7 laugher in 1980. They hadn't shut out the Pack since 1991.

Finally, rookie Devin Hester provided a sign of the flashy things to come when he brought back a punt 84 yards for the Bears' final touchdown. "The sky's the limit," cornerback Nathan Vasher said.

**SMASHED BY A TANK:** Brett Favre is dealt with rudely by defensive tackle **Tank Johnson.**
JIM PRISCHING

**GAME I** • SEPT. IO AT GREEN BAY

## BEARS 26 | PACKERS 0

**PIERSON RANKING** (entering game):

**REX-O-METER:** 18 of 26, 262 yards, I TD, I INT.
An excellent opener against a revered opponent increases optimism.

**233:** Number of games since the Packers had been shut out.

# SATISFACTION GUARANTEED

## Williams all mouth, not much football as Bears shut him up with thorough rout

THE BEARS were giggling into their sleeves at Detroit's Roy Williams after this one. The third-year wide receiver had guaranteed a Lions victory in Week 2 while bemoaning missed opportunities in a season-opening loss to Tampa Bay. But there was no mistaking these Bears for those Bucs as Rex Grossman established career highs with 289 passing yards and four TD passes and the Bears won in a walk. "When Rex is super hot like that, it's easy to play football," safety Mike Brown said.

Once again the tight end was more than an afterthought in the Bears' offense as Desmond Clark and John Gilmore combined for seven catches for 93 yards and three touchdowns, as many TD receptions as the Bears got from the tight end position in the entire 2005 season.

And once again the Bears' defense was dominant, sacking Lions quarterback Jon Kitna six times. Tank Johnson got him at the Lions' 3-yard line and forced a fumble in the first quarter, setting up the Bears' first touchdown. The Lions managed just 245 total yards and a third-quarter touchdown. They also lost three fumbles and piled up 104 yards on 14 penalties.

But the postgame talk was mostly about Grossman. He completed 20 of 27 throws and had a 71.7 completion percentage and a 128.7 passer rating after two games.

Roy Williams? Six catches for a quiet 71 yards. The Bears did all the talking—with their play on both sides of the ball.

**TUNING IN: Brendon Ayanbadejo and Brian Urlacher work on their dance steps after stopping Eddie Drummond on a fourth-quarter kickoff return.** NUCCIO DI NUZZO

GAME 2 • SEPT. 17 AT SOLDIER FIELD

| BEARS | 34 | LIONS | 7 |

**PIERSON RANKING** (entering game): ⑧

**6:** Number of Bears' sacks of Lions quarterback Jon Kitna.

**REX-O-METER:** 20 of 27, 289 yards, 4 TD, 0 INT. An explosive follow-up after an impressive opener.

PASSER RATING **148.0**

**DEFLECTED, REJECTED: Lions defensive back Jamar Fletcher knocks away a fourth-quarter pass intended for Mark Bradley.** JIM PRISCHING

**ARCHED SUPPORT:** Rashied Davis bends backward in jubilation after catching the winning 24-yard touchdown pass with 1:53 to play. JOHN SMIERCIAK

# A DENIAL ON DEFENSE

## Harris, Ogunleye turn tide as Bears survive in final minutes

**M**INNEAPOLIS' ear-splitting Metrodome might be Mike Ditka's least favorite venue on Earth, largely because the Bears have never had much success there. And they seemed headed for a fifth straight Metrodome defeat after Rex Grossman threw two interceptions and Ryan Longwell's third field goal had given the Vikings a 16-12 lead midway through the fourth quarter.

Bears fans might have been thinking a 2-1 start against NFC North teams wasn't too bad, what with two of the three games on the road and all. The Vikings were in run-out-the-clock mode when Tommie Harris nailed Chester Taylor in the Minnesota backfield as Taylor was taking Brad Johnson's handoff, forcing a fumble. Adewale Ogunleye recovered at the Vikings' 37-yard line with 3:25 remaining.

After a clutch third-down completion to Muhsin Muhammad, Grossman hit Rashied Davis for a 24-yard touchdown with 1:53 left, the first fourth-quarter TD pass of his career, lifting the Bears to an improbable third straight win.

It was not a pretty game. The Bears hurt themselves with seven penalties during a scoreless second quarter and 10 for the game. And Grossman handed the Vikings a go-ahead touchdown when he tossed an interception to Antoine Winfield deep in Bears territory early in the fourth quarter. But he shook it off and produced points on three of the Bears' last five possessions, including the biggest TD pass of his career.

**GAME 3 • SEPT. 24 AT MINNESOTA**

### BEARS 19    VIKINGS 16

**PIERSON RANKING (entering game):**
**7**

**4:** Robbie Gould field goals, essential as it took the Bears 58 minutes to score a TD.

**REX**-O-METER: 23 of 41, 278 yards, 1 TD, 2 INT. A winning effort, but some shakiness gives fans reasons to worry.

**64.9**

**HALF EMPTY: Muhsin Muhammad is brought down by Darren Sharper and Antoine Winfield on the final play of the first half. JIM PRISCHING**

**MINI-CONVOY: Charles Tillman (33) leads the way as Ricky Manning Jr. returns one of his two second-quarter interceptions.** JIM PRISCHING

# A PRIME-TIME SMASH

## Quarterly report looks bullish as 4th straight win starts Super Bowl chatter

**S**TATEMENT game? The Bears were so dominant in manhandling the defending NFC champion Seahawks that coach Lovie Smith had a hard time quelling Super Bowl talk after his team had completed a perfect "first quarter" of the season.

No such talk from Smith, of course.

"Tonight was our night," he said simply.

And it was, on both sides of the ball, as the Bears showed their stuff to a Sunday night national television audience in their first prime-time appearance of the season.

Rex Grossman surpassed 230 yards passing for the fourth straight game, completing 17 of 31 and throwing (ho-hum) two more touchdown passes. Thomas Jones pounded out 98 yards on the ground and scored the team's first two rushing touchdowns of the season.

And the defense preyed on a Seattle offense that was minus injured running back Shaun Alexander, the NFL's reigning MVP. The Bears limited the Seahawks to 77 rushing yards, and quarterback Matt Hasselbeck couldn't compensate. His 39.7 passer rating was the second lowest of his career. Hasselbeck threw two interceptions to Ricky Manning Jr. and was sacked five times, twice by rookie defensive end Mark Anderson, who blew past Walter Jones as if the All-Pro tackle's feet were encased in cement.

"We took it on the chin," Seattle coach Mike Holmgren said. "They were a load tonight, and they got us pretty good."

Dominant? The Bears' 37 points in this game were more than the 29 they had allowed in four games. That was the stingiest four-game stretch since 1937 for the NFC's lone remaining unbeaten team.

**SACK DANCE:** Tommie Harris struts after his fourth-quarter sack of Matt Hasselbeck, the Bears' fifth and final one of the night. JIM PRISCHING

**FACE-MASKED MAN:** Nathan Vasher takes a stiff arm in the chops from Maurice Morris in the third quarter. JOSÉ M. OSORIO

GAME 4 • OCT. I AT SOLDIER FIELD

## BEARS 37 SEAHAWKS 6

**PIERSON RANKING (entering game):**
⑤

**108:** Receiving yards for Bernard Berrian, including a 40-yard touchdown catch.

**REX-O-METER:** 17 of 31, 232 yards, 2 TD, 0 INT. Dominating performance against last season's Super Bowl runner-up.

**SMOKIN'? HARDLY:** Jason McKie and Justin Gage charge through a residue of fireworks before the Miami game—the Bears' first loss. CHARLES CHERNEY

# SECOND QUARTER

## GAMES 5-8

BILLS  CARDINALS  49ERS  DOLPHINS

**HAPPY HABIT:** Hester lights up with a smile after his 108-yard return of a missed field-goal attempt against the Giants. JIM PRISCHING

# DEVIN HESTER

## Dazzling special-teamer turns opponents in wrong direction

NORTH AND SOUTH. North and south. That was the message ringing in Devin Hester's ears as he ran onto the field that Monday night in October in Glendale, Ariz.

Bears special-teams coordinator Dave Toub wanted to be sure the rookie knew which direction to go, as if Hester ever needed a compass.

East, west, north, south, Hester's arrow has been pointing toward the end zone since his days at Suncoast High School in Riviera Beach, Fla., and the University of Miami, where he excelled on offense, defense and special teams. Coming to the Bears in the second round of the 2006 draft, Hester stayed the course his rookie season.

After returning a punt 84 yards for a touchdown in the Bears' victory over Green Bay in his first game as a pro, Hester struck again Oct. 16 with the Bears trailing Arizona 23-17 late in the fourth quarter.

En route to coming back from a 20-0 halftime deficit and still down 23-10 in the fourth quarter, the Bears urged Hester on

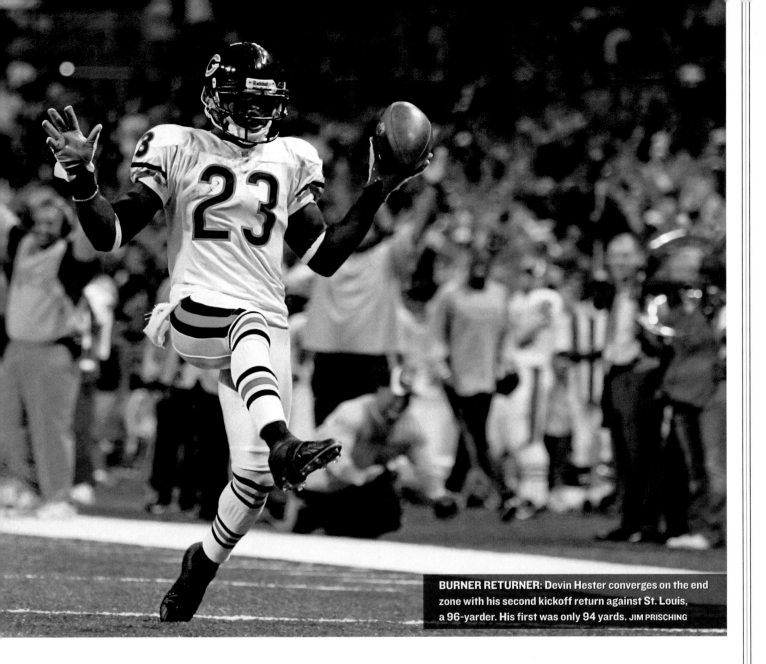

**BURNER RETURNER:** Devin Hester converges on the end zone with his second kickoff return against St. Louis, a 96-yarder. His first was only 94 yards. JIM PRISCHING

as he trotted onto the field to receive a punt, telling him, "We need a play."

Hester followed intstructions, followed his blockers and shot up the middle of the field for an 83-yard touchdown that became the game-winning score.

If the Bears didn't know by then they had a difference-maker in the 5-foot-11-inch, 189-pounder, they would soon enough. Hester completed a Pro Bowl and All-Pro season with a league-record six returns for touchdowns.

After breaking the 41-year-old team record for punt return yards in a game with his 152 against the Cardinals, Hester ripped off several more remarkable feats in the following weeks.

"Devin Hester is a guy who does whatev-er he wants to do," defensive tackle Tommie Harris said. "He's like a magic man."

Harris was referring to Hester's magic against the New York Giants three games later, in which he paused briefly in the end zone upon fielding a missed field goal before returning it 108 yards. That tied teammate Nathan Vasher's NFL record and paced the Bears to a 38-20 victory in the nationally televised Sunday night game.

Toub, who expected a pooch punt, watched Hester in the end zone, expecting him to down it for a touchback. "I was like the basketball coach saying, 'Don't shoot, don't shoot. Nice shot,'" he laughed.

Before he was through with his season, Hester also became the sixth player in NFL history to return two kickoffs for touchdowns in the same game while ringing up 249 return yards Dec. 11 at St. Louis. He finished the season with a league-leading 47 punt returns for 600 yards and was second in the NFL in punt-return average at 12.8.

Following the lead of his mentor, Deion Sanders, Hester doesn't need to be told which way to run anymore. Just point him to the end zone.

"I would say returning punts is 20 percent coaching and 80 percent natural instinct," Hester said. "You can't just put anybody out there. You feel when somebody is up on you, so you don't have to look. It's just something God blesses you with. And I have it."

— *Melissa Isaacson*

# JILTED AT HOMECOMING

## Jauron, Levy find no dance partners; rout is music to Bears' ears

**D**ICK JAURON was the Bears' coach from 1999-2003, but the team refused to show him any love on his return to Soldier Field, dominating his Bills on both sides of the ball. Buffalo general manager Marv Levy, a native Chicagoan, suffered through an equally dismal homecoming.

Willis McGahee came into the game as the NFL's leading rusher, but the Bears held him to 50 yards. They simply brutalized Bills quarterback J.P. Losman, limiting him to 115 yards and adding three interceptions and three sacks.

"It was a long day for us," Jauron acknowledged ruefully. "We made enough errors to let it get out of hand. It just snowballed."

On offense the Bears spread the wealth between their running and passing games. Thomas Jones surpassed 100 yards for the first time this season and Cedric Benson scored his first two touchdowns. Rex Grossman completed 15 of 27 passes for 182 yards and touchdowns to Bernard Berrian and Rashied Davis. Robbie Gould converted four more field goals, running his two-season streak to 17, and Brian Griese got into the act for the first time, completing four straight passes in mop-up duty.

The Bears were deprived of their second shutout of the season when a botched exchange led to a fourth-quarter fumble that Buffalo recovered and converted into its only touchdown. It hardly mattered against a Bears team averaging 31.2 points a game. And this statistic was telling: Their five-game output of 156 points matched the previous season's total after nine games.

**PLAYING THE ANGLES:** Terrence McGee (24) and Ko Simpson converge on Bernard Berrian on a 62-yard second-quarter catch. Simpson pushed him out of bounds. JIM PRISCHING

**GAME 5 • OCT. 8 AT SOLDIER FIELD**

**BEARS** 40 **BILLS** 7

**PIERSON RANKING** (entering game):

**REX-O-METER:** I5 of 27, I82 yards, 2 TD, 0 INT. Through five games, averaging two touchdown passes per game.

**145:** Total yards allowed to Buffalo, which came in averaging more than twice that at 295.5.

# DESERT STORM BLOWS IN

## Crown 'em: Defense, Hester erupt to save Grossman's tail

A BAD REX sighting. A Really Bad Rex sighting. Rex Grossman, who had scrupulously avoided turnovers in the Bears' five season-opening victories, turned the ball over six times as the Bears spotted Arizona a 20-point halftime lead that was still intact late in the third quarter.

But the defense and rookie Devin Hester bailed him out with a stirring "Miracle in the Desert" comeback.

The Bears finally scored in the third quarter, but Arizona matched their field goal and led 23-3 late in the period. That's when Brian Urlacher and the defense decided they'd better take over.

First Mark Anderson forced a Leinart fumble, which Mike Brown returned for a touchdown and a 23-10 score. Then Urlacher, who played the second half with maniacal intensity, stripped the ball from Edgerrin James, and Charles Tillman ran it in from 40 yards to cut it to 20-17. Finally, Hester fielded Scott Player's punt at his 17-yard line, slipped two tackles and blew past the rest of the Cardinals for an 83-yard touchdown return and a 24-23 lead with 2 minutes 58 seconds left.

Rookie QB Matt Leinart still had the

## BEARS 24 | CARDINALS 23

**PIERSON RANKING (entering game):**

❶ ○○○○○○○○○○○○○○○○○

**0:** Offensive touchdowns on a night when the Bears scored 24 points.

**REX-O-METER:** 14 of 37, 148 yards, 0 TD, 4 INT.

Is there a Griese in the house? Unconscionably poor game against a weak opponent.

**ROUTE 83: Devin Hester outruns Aaron Francisco, eluding the free safety's grasp on his game-winning 83-yard punt return.** JOHN SMIERCIAK

**BET ON IT: University of Phoenix Stadium was awash in Bears colors (right), and this fan was right on the money.** JIM PRISCHING

poise and the time to drive the Cardinals into position for a field-goal attempt, but Pro Bowler Neil Rackers' 40-yarder drifted wide right.

The Cardinals' collapse sparked a memorable postgame rant from coach Dennis Green: "The Bears are who we thought they were! And we let 'em off the hook!"

Lovie Smith had a different take: "Maybe we are a team of destiny."

**RACK IT UP:** Charles Tillman and Devin Hester go wild as Cardinals holder Scott Player leaves the field after Neil Rackers missed a potential game-winning field goal with **47** seconds left. JIM PRISCHING

**BIPLANE:** Muhsin Muhammad and Desmond Clark go airborne in celebration of one of Clark's two second-quarter touchdown receptions. JIM PRISCHING

**THREE OF A KIND: Rex Grossman (8) lines up a third-quarter pass to Desmond Clark (88).** JIM PRISCHING

# FINER THAN THE NINERS

## Grossman as good as gold in 1st half; defense wreaks havoc

THE BEARS were hoping Bad Rex would use the team's week off to disappear, and he did, at least for a while. The Rex Grossman who carved up the 49ers was as good as he had been in a Bears uniform, completing 23 of 29 passes for 252 yards, three touchdowns and a passer rating of 137.4.

Grossman was at his best in the first half while the Bears were pulling away, completing 16 of 18 in one stretch for 186 yards and three touchdowns.

Desmond Clark, the rejuvenated tight end, was Grossman's favorite target, catching six passes for 86 yards and two touch-downs. Muhsin Muhammad and Bernard Berrian caught five balls apiece as the Bears won by more than 25 points for the fifth time in seven games.

Grossman kept the 49ers guessing with play-action passes, and when the Bears did run, they did so effectively. Thomas Jones surpassed 100 yards for the second time.

Brian Urlacher's spectacular interception was the highlight of a defensive effort that blanked the 49ers for the first three quarters and held NFC rushing leader Frank Gore to 33 yards in the first half. Gore finished with 111 as the 49ers put 10 points on the board in the final period. But by then, Win No. 7 had gone into the books.

**GAME 7 • OCT. 29 AT SOLDIER FIELD**

| BEARS | 41 | 49ERS | 10 |
|-------|----|----|----|

**PIERSON RANKING (entering game):**
❶ ◯◯◯◯◯◯◯◯◯◯◯◯◯◯◯◯

**4:** Fumble recoveries by Tommie Harris, Israel Idonije, Ricky Manning Jr., Cameron Worrell.

**REX**-O-METER: 23 of 29, 252 yards, 3 TD, 0 INT. That's more like it: A Super Bowl team needs a Super Bowl quarterback.

FEEDING FRENZY: A host of Dolphins prepare to stack a Rex sandwich in the fourth quarter of their rout. CHARLES CHERNEY

# LAID OUT FLAT AS STREAK ENDS

## Plenty of blame to spread around in 1st loss

**GAME 8** • NOV. 5 AT SOLDIER FIELD

### DOLPHINS 31 BEARS 13

**PIERSON RANKING** (entering game):

❶ ② ③ ④ ⑤ ⑥ ⑦ ⑧ ⑨ ⑩ ⑪ ⑫ ⑬ ⑭ ⑮ ⑯

**3:** In each of these Bears stats: interceptions, sacks, fumbles lost.

**REX-O-METER:** 18 of 42, 210 yards, 1 TD, 3 INT. No way around it, a dreadful performance— but he isn't alone.

36.8

HIPS? CHECK: Brian Urlacher (left) and Alex Brown stare in disgust at the scoreboard.
JIM PRISCHING

THE 1972 Miami Dolphins were the last team to negotiate an NFL season undefeated, and surviving members gather to toast their achievement whenever the last unbeaten team goes down each season.

This year, as they had in 1985, they drank to their descendants. Bristling from criticism of its 1-6 record, an inspired, well-prepared Miami team forced the Bears into a litany of mistakes in putting a jarring end to their seven-game winning streak.

"Bad Rex" Grossman was the culprit in the eyes of most Bears fans, accounting for four of the six turnovers that the Dolphins converted into 28 points. The most telling: a pass right into the hands of Miami's Jason Taylor, which the All-Pro defensive end returned 20 yards for a second-quarter touchdown.

Devin Hester was guilty of an equally egregious fumble, mishandling a punt at his own 6-yard line that the Dolphins recovered and turned into a touchdown. Justin Gage also lost a fumble after replacing the injured Bernard Berrian at wide receiver.

The Bears defense had problems as well. Joey Harrington, a Bears nemesis in his Detroit days, threw three touchdown passes, at the conclusion of 6-, 12- and 24-yard "drives" set up by the turnovers. And there was no containing Dolphins running back Ronnie Brown, who rolled through the Bears for 157 yards on 29 carries.

"A tough day at the office," Lovie Smith said stoically.

It looked worse when Brian Urlacher limped off with a foot injury late in the game, but the Bears' inspirational leader was not hurt seriously and would not miss a game.

# BRIAN URLACHER

## Possessing sublime combination of talent, drive and leadership, he's Bears' bulwark

**BONNIE TRAFELET**

AFTER THE SAINTS' Reggie Bush pointed at Brian Urlacher during the final few steps of his 88-yard touchdown catch in the NFC championship game, somebody asked Urlacher his reaction.

On the Bears' sideline minutes after the play, that was obvious. The defense gathered, and Urlacher was one of several veterans incensed by what they had just seen Bush do. As any lip readers or fans near the front rows of Section 134 at Soldier Field can attest, the anger was real.

But the rage that fueled Urlacher and the Bears defense the rest of the way to their 39-14 victory had dissipated by the time the star linebacker addressed the issue at the postgame news conference.

"I think we're going to the Super Bowl," Urlacher said. It didn't bother him? Surely a rookie showing up one of the NFL's most respected players deserved the verbal equivalent of a forearm shiver, right?

"I'm sure they wish they had won the game instead of pointing at me," Urlacher answered.

He decided to take the high road to Miami. In those few sentences, in that capsule of a minute, Urlacher summarized the secret to the approach that has made him special over his seven seasons in Chicago: Only the Super Bowl matters.

It's always been a simple goal for the simplest of Bears. In Urlacher's one-track mind, the quest to reach the Super Bowl

always has superseded any concerns about being embarrassed by an opponent, about letting the media too close to his life outside of football, about considering himself anything other than one of 53 players on the payroll despite his once-in-a-generation athletic ability.

Some players might have pouted about finishing fourth in the NFL Defensive Player of the Year voting, especially when the player who finished third, Shawne Merriman, had been suspended after testing positive for steroids. Urlacher shrugged.

The one marquee player in the locker room also made it known he would be willing to rework his contract if the Bears thought it necessary in their attempt to keep fellow linebacker Lance Briggs.

Ask Urlacher about finishing with 185 tackles, the second-highest total of his career. Ask him about the freakishly athletic play he made against San Francisco, deflecting a pass while being blocked and making a one-handed interception while still engaged with the offensive lineman. Ask him about the fourth-quarter strip of Arizona's Edgerrin James that probably only Dick Butkus could match in the category of most dominant performance by a Bears linebacker.

Ask Urlacher anything about himself, and the answer changes as much as his monotone voice. The Bears' most outstanding player since Walter Payton cares little

about individual achievements, and that might seem phony or contrived if he hadn't been the same way since entering the league in 2000.

"This overshadows everything," Urlacher said when asked to compare playing in a Super Bowl with winning the NFL defensive MVP. "This is why we play the game, to get to the Super Bowl."

That has been Urlacher's mantra since his rookie year, but only this season did the Bears build a team around him capable of producing results to match his rhetoric. Over his first six seasons, the Bears were 45-51 and lost home playoff games after winning the NFC North in 2001 and '05.

But Urlacher sensed this season would be different as early as training camp. That's when he laid out a Super Bowl-or-bust standard and revealed what drives him by saying, "I know I need that ring."

That was the urgency Urlacher brought

to the league when he arrived from New Mexico as a free safety who always played harder because he felt he was learning the job of linebacker. That was the urgency Urlacher instilled in the defense at the beginning of this special season, and the urgency with which the defensive players took the field after Bush's senseless taunt.

The Saints never scored another point.

"We knew what we had to do to win, and we went out and did it," Urlacher said.

WE knew what WE had to do to win, and WE went out and did it.

He really should change the spelling of his first name. As much as any season, this one confirmed there is definitely no I in Brian Urlacher, Bears superstar.

—*David Haugh*

**ONWARD, UPWARD: Quarterbacking the defense and finishing with 185 tackles, Brian Urlacher led the Bears to Miami.** NUCCIO DI NUZZO

**STEADY HANDS:** With a two-year record of 24-8 and two NFC North titles, Lovie Smith has shown exemplary leadership. HEATHER STONE

# THIRD QUARTER

## GAMES 9-12

GIANTS  JETS  PATRIOTS  VIKINGS

**A WATCHFUL WAY: Tommie Harris focuses from the sideline against the Giants. JIM PRISCHING**

# TOMMIE HARRIS

## After devastating injuries, Pro Bowler has leg up on next season

ONE OF TOMMIE HARRIS' many rare talents is singing the gospel. With a little prompting and gentle coaxing, the 6-foot-3-inch, 295-pound Texas native will belt out a spiritual rendition that will inspire listeners.

The gospel truth is that the Bears truly missed their Pro Bowl defensive tackle after he suffered season-ending injuries to his left knee and hamstring, forcing him out of the last four regular-season games and the playoffs.

Harris was hurt Dec. 3, early in the second half of the division-clinching victory over the Vikings, when he tackled running back Chester Taylor.

"It's actually better to do what I did than to have a cut or torn hamstring," Harris said. "I didn't tear my hamstring. It's just the tendon, and it has been reattached."

The injury happened on the second play of the third quarter. After Harris tackled Taylor, he was unable to get up. He said afterward he felt like he had done "the splits." He was carted into the locker room and left the stadium on crutches and with a plastic cast on his left leg.

Harris had become the target of nearly constant double teams as offenses recog-

nized him as a disruptive force inside. He had been a stellar member of a stout defensive front that had just completed a rugged three-game East Coast swing by going 2-1 against the highly regarded Giants, Jets and Patriots, outscoring them 61-37.

Because of the team's depth at defensive tackle, players such as Tank Johnson, Ian Scott and Alfonso Boone began to see significant playing time. But the impact of not having Harris to stop the run and pressure quarterbacks was felt mightily.

"We'll miss Tommie a lot," defensive end Alex Brown said when Harris went out. "We

have guys who can play the position, but you can't replace Tommie."

Said coach Lovie Smith: "No one in the league has a player like Tommie Harris."

And general manager Jerry Angelo said: "It's a tough loss, given that Tommie's a Pro Bowl player. Anytime you lose a player of his quality, it's going to affect your team. But the good news is we have good experience at the position and feel real good about the [other] players. We've just got to keep finding a way, and I feel very confident we will."

Raised in Killeen, Texas, Harris became one of the nation's top high school defensive prospects. He also starred on the track team as a shot putter.

At the University of Oklahoma, Harris won the Lombardi Trophy as the nation's top lineman in 2003.

A man of principle, Harris refused to take part in the Playboy Magazine All-America team photo shoot.

"I have four sisters and no interest in promoting Hugh Hefner's agenda," said Harris, whose father, Tommie Sr., is a Pentecostal minister. "What would I be saying by being in that magazine? That I'm poor and looking for publicity?"

The 14th pick of the 2004 draft, Harris finished second in the balloting for defensive rookie of the year. He made the NFC Pro Bowl team in his second season and earned comparisons to veteran standout Warren Sapp.

In his first four games of 2006, Harris recorded five sacks and earned NFC Player of the Week honors twice. Despite the injury, Harris looks forward to returning next season.

"I want … to be able to … come out of my stance again, run and do what I know I can do," he said.

—*Fred Mitchell*

**A SUPPORTER'S SUPPORT: On crutches, Harris gives advice to Tank Johnson in the semifinal win over the Seahawks.**
JOHN SMIERCIAK

**HARRIED BY HARRIS: Seattle's Matt Hasselbeck feels Harris' pressure in the Bears' October victory.**
JOSÉ M. OSORIO

# BEARS' SILVER BULLET: HESTER'S NIGHT MOVE

## 108-yard return gives Giants mystery without any clues

THE BEARS unveiled an impressive arsenal of weapons in running their record under the lights to 5-0 in coach Lovie Smith's three seasons.

Rex Grossman got off to a shaky start, but he threw a 29-yard touchdown strike to Mark Bradley 25 seconds before halftime. Grossman finished with 18 completions in 30 attempts for 246 yards and three touchdowns. Bradley, replacing the injured Bernard Berrian at wide receiver, set up another touchdown with a 38-yard grab in the fourth quarter.

Wet weather and a comfortable lead pushed the Bears toward a ball-control strategy, and Thomas Jones helped them implement it by running for 113 yards, his third 100-yard game of the season.

But the play of the game occurred on special teams. The Bears led 24-20 early in the fourth quarter when the Giants' Jay Feely lined up for a 52-yard field-goal attempt. He was well short, and Devin Hester fielded the ball deep in his end zone. The swift rookie hesitated, then brought the ball out at his teammates' urging. Hester beat the first wave of tacklers to

DIVE BOMBERS: R.W. McQuarters (25) and Gibril Wilson flatten Thomas Jones. JIM PRISCHING

GAME 9 • NOV. 12 AT EAST RUTHERFORD, N.J.

| BEARS | 38 | GIANTS | 20 |
|-------|----|--------|----|

**PIERSON RANKING (entering game):**
① ② ③ ④ **⑤** ⑥ ⑦ ⑧ ⑨ ⑩ ⑪ ⑫ ⑬ ⑭ ⑮ ⑯

**123:** Receiving yardage of Muhsin Muhammad, exactly half of Grossman's total.

**REX-O-METER:** 18 of 30, 246 yards, 3 TD, 1 INT. Some satisfaction for fans as Grossman shows the ability to rebound from a slow start.

105.7

the sideline, where a convoy of blockers led by Charles Tillman, Hunter Hillenmeyer and Brendon Ayanbadejo escorted him on a 108-yard touchdown return, matching the record teammate Nathan Vasher had set when he brought back a missed field goal 108 yards against the 49ers in the 2005 season.

"Devin Hester is a playmaker," special-teams coordinator Dave Toub said. "He's going to make more good plays than bad ones."

**HOLD THE CATCH-UP:** Devin Hester glides into the end zone unscathed after his 108-yard return. SCOTT STRAZZANTE

**DAVID, MEET GOLIATH: Giants receiver David Tyree absorbs a huge hit from Brian Urlacher.** JIM PRISCHING

**TEMPORARY HELP:** Charles Tillman scoots off after recovering a fumble against the Giants, only to fumble it right back later in the play. **JIM PRISCHING**

# JETS' PURSUIT IS POINTLESS

## Defense cracks down in 2nd shutout

THE BEARS reverted to their Black and Blue Division heritage in completing a sweep of New York. On a wet, windy day at the Meadowlands, the defenses slugged it out, and the Bears prevailed with their second shutout of the season.

Brian Urlacher had a spectacular game, making 11 tackles all over the field and de-

nying the Jets their best scoring opportunity with an end-zone interception. Strong safety Todd Johnson, replacing the injured Mike Brown, matched Urlacher's 11 tackles, and Nathan Vasher intercepted a Chad Pennington pass.

"They are as good as advertised," Jets running back Leon Washington said of the Bears defense.

On offense, the Bears did just enough

to win. Turning a bit of Jets trickeration against them, the Bears recovered an onside kick to open the second half. That set up Robbie Gould's field goal, his 24th in a row, for the first points of the game.

Both quarterbacks had trouble throwing in the elements, but Rex Grossman was efficient, completing 11 of 22 for 119 yards and the game's only touchdown, a 57-yarder to Mark Bradley. More importantly, Grossman did not throw an interception.

The ground was the way to travel this week, and the Bears had a productive trip, gaining a season-high 173 rushing yards. Thomas Jones had 121 on 23 carries, his third 100-yard game in four weeks, and Cedric Benson added 51 on 10 tries.

"You have to run the ball," offensive coordinator Ron Turner said. "If you're one-dimensional, you're in trouble."

**SUFFOCATION CITY:** Nathan Vasher and Danieal Manning (38) hammer Laveranues Coles.

**GAME 10 • NOV. 19 AT EAST RUTHERFORD, N.J.**

## BEARS 10 JETS 0

**PIERSON RANKING** (entering game):

**2**

**4.9:** Bears rushing average, a full yard better than the Jets.

**REX**-O-**METER:** 11 of 22, 119 yards, 1 TD, 0 INT. A steady if unspectacular day, but more than enough to win.

**81.4**

**MARKING HIS SPOT:** Receiver Mark Bradley sprints to the end zone on a 57-yard pass from Rex Grossman in the fourth quarter. JOSÉ M. OSORIO

# EASTWARD, HO: 2 OF 3 NOT BAD

## Patriots, Samuel bring end to road success

**WAY IN THE WAY:** Artrell Hawkins' 45-yard pass-interference penalty on Bernard Berrian (80) set up Cedric Benson's touchdown three plays later. JIM PRISCHING

O N THEIR third trip east in as many weeks, the Bears got a look at what they aspire to be. New England, winner of three of the last five Super Bowls, made the plays that had to be made in handing the Bears their first road loss after five victories.

The big disparity was at quarterback. The Patriots sacked Rex Grossman just once, but they were in his face all afternoon and pressured him into another rough day: 15-for-34, 176 yards and a 23.7 passer rating. Cornerback Asante Samuel intercepted him three times, and Grossman lost a fumble.

Tom Brady, meanwhile, was a study in cool precision, passing for 267 yards and a touchdown. Brady was most impressive on third down, completing seven of 12 passes for 116 yards and keeping alive a scoring drive with an 11-yard scramble on third down on which he artfully eluded Brian Urlacher.

The Bears had more success running the ball, Thomas Jones gaining 99 yards on 23 carries and Cedric Benson adding 46 yards on 10 trips. Benson scored their only touchdown on a 2-yard run in the fourth quarter.

Robbie Gould kicked two field goals but had his streak of successful kicks halted at 26 when the Pats' Richard Seymour blocked his 45-yard attempt in the first quarter.

The Bears had a final chance when Alex Brown recovered Corey Dillon's fumble at the Bears' 22-yard line with just over a minute remaining, but Samuel stepped in front of Bernard Berrian for a spectacular game-saving interception.

**GAME II • NOV. 26 AT FOXBORO, MASS.**

| PATRIOTS 17 | BEARS 13 |
|---|---|

**PIERSON RANKING (entering game):**

**II:** Yards gained by Tom Brady when he juked Urlacher, leading to the winning score.

**REX-O-METER:** 15 of 34, 176 yards, 0 TD, 3 INT. He'll be seeing Asante Samuel in his nightmares.

**CURSES:** Bernard Berrian lets loose a bit of frustration after an incompletion in the first quarter, but he had a good day with five catches for 104 yards. NUCCIO DI NUZZO

STEAMED: Brian Urlacher zeroes in on Brad Johnson, who was harassed into four interceptions and a 10.3 passer rating. JIM PRISCHING

# DOWNPLAYING DOWNSIDE

## Quarterback play poor, Harris injured, but Bears clinch NFC North

THE BEARS clinched their second straight NFC North title on a day when their offense barely showed up. And their quarterback probably wished he had stayed in bed.

It was a cold, windy, brutal day for passing, and Rex Grossman fell victim to the conditions, completing just 6 of 19 for 34 yards with three interceptions and an abysmal passer rating of 1.3.

Fortunately for the Bears, Minnesota counterpart Brad Johnson wasn't much better, throwing for 73 yards with four interceptions for an unsightly 10.3 passer rating. During one third-quarter stretch, Johnson threw four passes, and three were intercepted.

"That's usually enough to get you beat," Vikings coach Brad Childress said.

The Bears managed just 83 yards rushing. What saved them were big plays from the defense and special teams. Ricky Manning Jr., back from a one-game league suspension, brought back an interception 54 yards for a touchdown. And Devin Hester, expanding his role as one of the Bears' most potent weapons, scored on a 45-yard punt return.

The Bears' celebration of their NFC North title was muted. Tommie Harris, a dominant defensive tackle all season, limped off with a severe hamstring injury and would miss the rest of the season.

And Vikings safety Darren Sharper might have been speaking for all of Chicago when he said, "The Bears have to be asking themselves if this is the quarterback who can take them where they want to go."

## BEARS 23 VIKINGS 13

**PIERSON RANKING** (entering game):

**11.6:** Combined passer rating for the two starting quarterbacks.

**REX-O-METER:** 6 of 19, 34 yards, 0 TD, 3 INT. Can it get any worse? Unfortunately, yes.

**DARTIN' DEVIN:** Devin Hester (left) skips past his Minnesota pursuers as he scores on a 45-yard punt return in the first quarter.
**CHARLES CHERNEY**

**CORNER POCKET:** Cedric Benson tucks the ball just inside the pylon, scoring past Darren Sharper in the third quarter.
**JIM PRISCHING**

**FRIGHTFUL FINISH:** Tank Johnson's off-the-field problems complicated the Bears' slide at season's end. JOHN SMIERCIAK

# FOURTH QUARTER

## GAMES 13-16

RAMS  BUCCANEERS  LIONS  PACKERS

# ROBBIE GOULD

## Bears ride The Mayor's coattails to landslide victory in NFC

THEY CALL Robbie Gould "The Mayor," which embarrasses him yet fits him. Candidates could do worse than to run a campaign on Gould's energy and use of the word "awesome."

But as engaging as Gould is, his teammates care considerably more about his productivity, which during the 2006 season was just short of perfect. He:

● Was second in the NFL in scoring with 143 points.

● Became the first Bears kicker since Kevin Butler in 1986 to lead the NFC in scoring.

● Set team records of 24 consecutive field goals to start the season, 26 dating back to the '05 season, at least one field goal in 22 straight games and an 88.9 percent success rate.

● Had a 49-yard game-winner over Seattle in the first round of the playoffs and 13 points in the NFC championship victory over New Orleans, including field goals from 19, 43 and 24 yards.

Working construction in his hometown of Lock Haven, Pa., after being waived by his favorite boyhood team, the New England Patriots, and then the Baltimore Ravens, Gould signed with the Bears after a tryout in October 2005.

"This is the place that gave me an opportunity," said Gould, a soccer player as a boy before kicking a football regularly for the first time his sophomore year in high school and then walking on at Penn State. "And

**THAT'S THE POINT: Gould acknowledges the crowd after booting his first extra point in the NFC semifinal against Seattle.** JOHN SMIERCIAK

you're always going to hold a special place in your heart for the first team that gives you an opportunity, like I do with New England. I'm sure a lot of my teammates get tired of me talking about the Patriots, but they gave me my first opportunity. The Chicago Bears gave me the real opportunity and chance to play, and I'm very grateful for that."

Grateful but not unrealistic. The life of a kicker is fraught with uncertainty, and

Gould reminds himself of this often.

"It's a performance-based business, and either you do it or you don't," said Gould, who never had a kicking coach until he got to the NFL. "With kickers, there's no in between. And if you don't, there's going to be somebody else sitting in your shoes, doing your interviews, making your kicks and taking your reps."

Until then, and Bears fans have a hard time imagining that will ever happen, Gould continues to be one of the most popular players in the locker room, not necessarily a politician but always The Mayor.

"At the end of the day you are a kicker—you can't change that," Gould said. "It's just one of those things that you don't mean as much as maybe the rest of the guys do and you have a little bit more down time than they do, but I think Brad [Maynard] and I do a very good job of breaking every stereotype from not being athletic to not being a guy who fits in the locker room."

A disciple of All-Pro Adam Vinatieri when he was with New England, Gould nearly met the Patriots in the Super Bowl. Instead, he met Vinatieri and the Colts. But nothing could take away from his experience.

"Everything up to this point of my career has happened so fast, I don't think I've really had a chance to digest any of it," Gould said. "Hopefully one day I will, maybe at the end of 15 years, maybe at the end of a three-year career. You never know."

—*Melissa Isaacson*

**WRONG FOOT ...: But right idea as Gould counts down the final seconds of the NFC championship game.** NUCCIO DI NUZZO

# DOUBLE DOSE OF DEVIN

## 94-, 96-yard returns leave even his teammates slack-jawed

WHEN the Bears' 2006 season is put in historical perspective, the "Devin Hester Game" will merit significant mention.

On a night when the Bears rediscovered their passing game, the defense was solid and the running game was efficient, Hester provided the spark that marked his team as something special not once, but twice.

In the second quarter, while it was still a ballgame, Hester ran back a kickoff 94 yards for a touchdown, setting a team record with his fifth TD return of the season.

Early in the fourth quarter, after the Rams had driven 89 yards for a touchdown to creep back into the game and put the Bears' defense on its heels, Hester raced 96 yards with the ensuing kickoff for another touchdown, setting an NFL record.

Hester's heroics not only demoralized the Rams, they energized his team and mesmerized the Edward Jones Dome crowd and the "Monday Night Football" TV audience.

"I've never seen anything like it in my life," teammate Brian Urlacher said.

To Hester, it was just another day at the office. He was more excited by the opportunity to play defensive back after Nathan Vasher and Todd Johnson were injured.

"When you get your hands on the ball, you want to make something happen," Hester said.

That was Rex Grossman's mantra as well. The mercurial quarterback bounced back from a rough outing to complete 13 of 23 passes for 200 yards and two touchdowns with no turnovers. The Bears piled up 372 yards of offense, 171 of it in an explosive third quarter.

**BROWN OUT: Muhsin Muhammad grabs a 14-yard touchdown pass over the Rams' Fakhir Brown in the third quarter. JIM PRISCHING**

**GAME 13** • DEC. 11 AT ST. LOUIS

| BEARS | 42 | RAMS | 27 |
|-------|----|----|----|

**PIERSON RANKING (entering game):**
**4**

**REX-O-METER:** 13 of 23, 200 yards, 2 TD, 0 INT. A very nice effort that will be forever overshadowed by Hester's night.

**28:** Consecutive points Bears ran off from 13-7 deficit to 35-13 fourth-quarter lead.

**EDWARD JONES DOOM:** Devin Hester gestures toward his pursuers as he concludes his 96-yard kickoff return. CHARLES CHERNEY

# PASSING FANCY IN OVERTIME WIN

## Grossman overshadows Tank's trouble

**A**FTER ENDURING the most tumultuous week of their season off the field, the Bears needed every point the offense could muster to hold off surprisingly stubborn Tampa Bay. And they had to work overtime to do it.

Three days earlier, defensive tackle Tank Johnson had been arrested after a police raid at his suburban home turned up unregistered firearms. Two nights after that, Johnson and boyhood friend Willie B. Posey were at a Chicago nightspot when Posey was shot and killed after a dispute on the dance floor.

Johnson was held out of the Tampa Bay game, joining injured fellow starters Tommie Harris and Mike Brown on the sidelines. The Buccaneers took advantage of the Bears' depleted defense as journeyman quarterback Tim Rattay passed for 268 yards and three touchdowns after replacing overmatched rookie Bruce Gradkowski.

But Rex Grossman was even better, completing 29 of 44 passes for 339 yards and two touchdowns. Grossman's career-high yardage total represented the first 300-yard passing day by a Bears QB in more than four years. Four receivers caught at least five passes, Desmond Clark grabbing seven for a career-high 125 yards,

**NO HOLD BARRED: Robbie Gould grabs holder Brad Maynard to celebrate the kicker's game-winning field goal.** NUCCIO DI NUZZO

the first 100-yard receiving day by a Bears tight end in 21 years.

Grossman's best throw of the day might well have been a third-and-8, 28-yard strike to Rashied Davis to the Tampa Bay 20-yard line. That set up Robbie Gould's game-winning field goal in overtime.

"I felt comfortable in the pocket, confident in my reads and in the game plan and confident in my approach," Grossman said.

**GAME 14 • DEC. 17 AT SOLDIER FIELD**

| BEARS | 34 | BUCS | 31 |
|-------|----|----|----|

**PIERSON RANKING** (entering game):

 **104.3**

**REX-O-METER:** 29 of 44, 339 yards, 2 TD, 0 INT.
He is outstanding on a day the Bears desperately need him to be.

**193:** Grossman's passing yards to non-wide receivers (TEs Clark, Gilmore; RBs Jones, McKie).

**PIT STOP:** Brian Urlacher (54) and Lance Briggs barrel into Michael Pittman simultaneously to blow up a running play. JIM PRISCHING

**THE BREAKUP:** Bears cornerback Charles Tillman strains to extend his left arm and knock down a pass intended for Tampa Bay's Joey Galloway in the third quarter. NUCCIO DI NUZZO

**SLIPSHOD:** With Stanley Wilson defending, Bernard Berrian just misses cradling a third-quarter pass. JIM PRISCHING

# JUST ENOUGH FUEL LEFT

## Gould drives it home as Lions' last-play bid sputters in Motor City

THE BEARS' visit to the Motor City for their final road test of the season was successful on three levels: They rested some injured starters, they played some little-used backups and they won the game.

Robbie Gould, the former Penn State kicker who was signed off a construction crew in 2005, celebrated his ascension to Pro Bowl status by going 4-for-4 on field goals, including a 39-yarder that gave the Bears the lead late in the fourth quarter. His 44-yarder a little over two minutes later left the Lions needing a touchdown to win.

They almost got one, but butterfingered Mike Williams failed to corral Jon Kitna's desperation heave to the end zone on the final play.

Gould set a franchise record with 32 field goals in a season and found himself sharing the postgame laurels with backup quarterback Brian Griese, who directed the Bears on their last two field-goal drives.

The first one was particularly impressive. Griese replaced Rex Grossman with the Bears pinned at their 7-yard line and completed his first three passes, later hooking up with Mark Bradley for 16 yards on a third-and-9 play. Gould's go-ahead field goal capped a 12-play, 72-yard advance. His fourth came after Mark Anderson sacked Kitna and forced a fumble, which the Bears recovered in Detroit territory.

Grossman was a credible 20-for-36 for 197 yards and a touchdown before turning it over to Griese. Ten Bears caught passes, including Muhsin Muhammad, who snagged the 700th of his career.

The Bears' 7-1 road record was their best since 1986.

**GOING FORTH:** Robbie Gould follows through on one of his three fourth-quarter field goals, which provided the margin of victory. JIM PRISCHING

**A LOVIE TAP:** Coach Lovie Smith pats Adrian Peterson's helmet after the running back's 2-yard touchdown. JIM PRISCHING

**GAME 15 · DEC. 24 AT DETROIT**

| BEARS | 26 | LIONS | 21 |
|---|---|---|---|

**PIERSON RANKING (entering game):**
2

**22:** Yardage of pass from Kitna to Mike Williams that would have won on final play.

**REX-O-METER:** 20 of 36, 197 yards, 1 TD, 0 INT. An acceptable showing in a meaningless game that allows Griese ample playing time.

PASSER RATING 80.4

**GRABBING AIR: Devin Hester muffs a third-quarter punt. Fortunately, Cameron Worrell recovered.** JOSÉ M. OSORIO

# AN EARLY HANGOVER

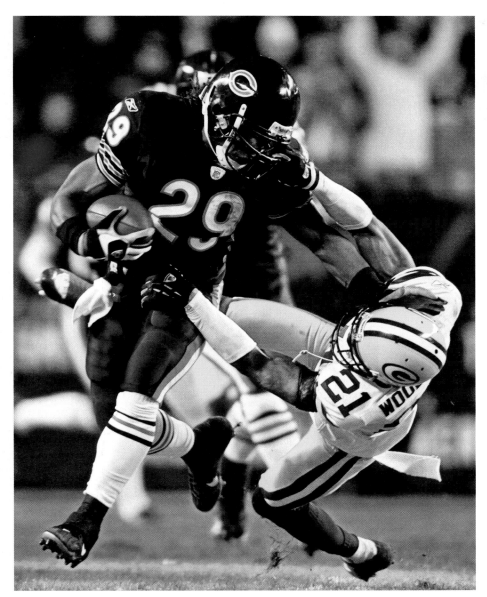

**HAND-TO-HAND COMBAT:** Adrian Peterson stiff-arms Charles Woodson as he picks up 37 yards on a fake punt in the third quarter. JIM PRISCHING

## 'Meaningless' or not, aspirin needed after New Year's Eve game produces headaches

**S**O MUCH for momentum heading into the playoffs.

The adjective "meaningless" was applied to this regular-season finale so often that the Bears appeared to buy into the description. Not even NBC's decision to move the game to prime time in case it was Brett Favre's finale could rescue the Bears from their torpor. Long-faced Bears fans were in no mood to celebrate New Year's Eve after their playoff-bound team was embarrassed by a Packers squad whose modest goal was a .500 finish.

The evening started poorly for the Bears and got worse. Rex Grossman completed more passes to the Packers (three) than the Bears (two), and he lost a fumble in a desultory first half in which he achieved a 0.0 passer rating. Two of Grossman's three interceptions were returned for touchdowns.

Brian Griese took over in the second half and connected with Mark Bradley on a 75-yard touchdown pass, but Griese didn't move the team any better than Grossman had and threw two interceptions.

The Bears' most effective passer was punter Brad Maynard, who completed a 37-yarder to Adrian Peterson on a fake punt. If Favre were contemplating retirement, he probably had second thoughts after shredding the Bears for 285 yards and a touchdown, running his career record against them to 22-8.

"We didn't have the sense of urgency," Grossman said. "Everything that could go wrong did go wrong."

Not exactly what Bears fans wanted to hear heading into the playoffs. Fortunately, the Bears had a bye week to work out their problems.

---

**GAME 16 • DEC. 31 AT SOLDIER FIELD**

**PACKERS 26 BEARS 7**

**PIERSON RANKING** (entering game):
❷

PASSER RATING
0.0

**REX-O-METER:** 2 of 12, 33 yards, 0 TD, 3 INT.
Abysmal. Wretched. Miserable. Contemptible. Shall we go on?

**0.0:** Grossman's passer rating. It can't get any worse.

**VERY SPECIAL-TEAMERS:** Kicker Robbie Gould leaps into the arms of holder Brad Maynard after Gould's game-winning field goal against the Seahawks. NUCCIO DI NUZZO

# OVERTIME

## CONFERENCE PLAYOFFS

SEAHAWKS  SAINTS

## SUPER BOWL

COLTS

**FINISHING KICK:** Robbie Gould's winning field goal in overtime gives the Bears a 27-24 victory over Seattle in the **NFC** semifinal. JIM PRISCHING

*By* JOHN MULLIN

# GOULD-PLATED

## Kicker ties it in regulation, then beats Seahawks in overtime

THE BEARS' string of home-field disasters in the playoffs ended when Seattle came to Soldier Field for the second time in the 2006 season. The Seahawks' dream of a second straight Super Bowl appearance was dashed when Robbie Gould kicked a 41-yard field goal to tie the game in regulation, then won it with a 49-yarder on the Bears' first possession of overtime.

First-round byes hadn't helped after the 2001 or 2005 seasons, when the Bears lost their home playoff openers to Philadelphia and Carolina, respectively. But with Rex Grossman passing for 282 yards, the offense scored touchdowns on two of its first three possessions.

Thomas Jones finished an 80-yard drive after the opening kickoff with a 9-yard touchdown run. After Seattle scored on Matt Hasselbeck's pass to Nate Burleson on the first play of the second quarter, Grossman needed just one play to answer with a 68-yard strike to Bernard Berrian, the longest play in each player's career.

"People always talk about managing the game," center Olin Kreutz said. "Well, if we had a quarterback who managed the game, we wouldn't have come close to winning the game. That's why we like Rex so much. He's not there to just manage the game. He's there to win games, and we think we need him to win the Super Bowl, so that's why he's here."

**GUARDING ANGEL: Thomas Jones follows left guard Ruben Brown into the end zone to put the Bears ahead 21-14 at halftime.** JOHN SMIERCIAK

The Seahawks tied the game on a 4-yard touchdown run by Shaun Alexander after Grossman fumbled as he was being sacked at the Bears' 26. But Grossman completed passes of 21 yards to Muhsin Muhammad and 18 yards to Rashied Davis, setting up Jones for a 7-yard scoring run and a 21-14 halftime lead.

Seattle closed within 21-17 on Josh

**NFC SEMIFINAL**
JAN. 14 AT SOLDIER FIELD

## BEARS 27 SEAHAWKS 24

**11:** Tackles by Lance Briggs, including stop of tight end Will Heller 2 yards short of first down on Seattle's last gain of overtime.

**REX-O-METER:** 21 of 38, 282 yards, 1 TD, 1 INT. Produces several big plays, and only interception hit Muhammad in the hands.

Brown's field goal on its first possession of the second half and took the lead when Alexander blew through the middle of the defense for 13 yards and a 24-21 edge with five minutes to play in the third quarter.

That was the Seahawks' final score. Grossman and Cedric Benson led the Bears on a 48-yard drive to set up Gould's tying kick, and Tank Johnson sacked Hasselbeck to move Seattle out of field-goal range and force overtime.

The Seahawks failed to get into Bears territory in overtime. Israel Idonije then rushed Ryan Plackemeier into a shanked punt that gave the Bears the ball at their 34. Grossman converted a third-and-10 to Davis, and Gould lived up to his All-Pro status with the fourth game-winning field goal of his career.

The Bears piled up 371 yards despite losing 31 on three sacks of Grossman.

"It's a monkey off our back to get that win," linebacker Brian Urlacher said.

**RINGED AROUND THE COLLAR: Alex Brown helps make Matt Hasselbeck's day miserable, sacking him in the second quarter.** JIM PRISCHING

**FLIGHT CONTROL:** Brian Urlacher (54) and Chris Harris go airborne and crash the passing lane to break up a second-quarter pass intended for **Darrell Jackson.** SCOTT STRAZZANTE

*By* JOHN MULLIN

# SINFULLY SIMPLE

## Punishing run game, effective defense lift Bears past Saints, on to Super Bowl

**THE ENTERTAINER:** Cedric Benson shakes off the tackle of Josh Bullocks to score in the fourth quarter of the NFC title game.
**JOHN SMIERCIAK**

THE PLAYOFF monkey off their backs, the Bears stood up straight all the way and destroyed the New Orleans Saints 39-14 in the NFC championship game to reach the second Super Bowl in franchise history.

The 39 points represented the third-highest total ever put up in an NFC title game and was even more notable because, as players were quick to point out, it was New Orleans, America's adopted team in the wake of Hurricane Katrina, that supposedly had the better offense.

"The Saints were a great story," linebacker Hunter Hillenmeyer said. "But we're glad their season ended here."

The Bears made sure the story ended their way, forcing four turnovers, sacking Drew Brees three times and rushing for 196 yards and three touchdowns as they scored more than 30 points for the eighth time in 18 games.

A sprinkling of snow and generally dismal weather made the footing shaky at times. But Thomas Jones, who scored twice and rushed for 123 yards with an average of 6.5 yards per carry, said:

"It couldn't have been a more perfect situation than this for Chicago Bears football.

It's snowing, [we're] running the football, our defense is playing hard, getting turnovers, making some big hits. I mean, this is just the perfect situation for us."

The defense forced three fumbles in the first quarter and recovered two, but the Bears put up only three Robbie Gould field goals as the offense stalled. However, Jones made it look like a looming blowout when he carried on all eight plays of a 69-yard touchdown drive in the second quarter, making it 16-0.

New Orleans answered with a touchdown pass to rookie Marques Colston just before halftime and shook Reggie Bush loose for an 88-yard catch-and-run TD to trim it to

**NFC CHAMPIONSHIP** • JAN. 21 AT SOLDIER FIELD

## BEARS 39 SAINTS 14

**196:** Bears rushing yardage behind an offensive line that allowed zero sacks.

PASSER RATING
**73.2**

**REX-O-METER:** 11 of 26, 144 yards, 1 TD, 0 INT.
Stats not eye-popping, but his decisions, and final score, are.

16-14 less than three minutes into the second half. However, Bush taunted pursuing linebacker Brian Urlacher and added to the insult by somersaulting into the end zone. Bush immediately apologized to coach Sean Payton but should have done that to the Bears, who were left fuming. The Saints never got close to the Bears' end zone again.

A forced intentional grounding by Brees in the end zone gave the Bears a safety late in the third quarter, and the offense scored on three of its first four possessions in the fourth quarter, a tumbling 33-yard catch by Bernard Berrian preceding runs by Cedric Benson and Jones. The Bears closed with 23 unanswered points.

The locker room was a happy place

**AT ARM'S LENGTH:**
Thomas Jones applies a
stiff-arm to Josh Bullocks
on the second-quarter
drive in which Jones
carried eight straight
times, ending with a
touchdown.
NUCCIO DI NUZZO

after clearing another obstacle in a season
defined by the chant of "Super Bowl!" after practices. But there were no wild cel-
ebrations, no beverage showers, no victory
cigars. Perhaps because in some Bears'
minds, they hadn't won anything yet.

"We haven't," cornerback Charles
Tillman insisted. "Today we're one step
closer to attaining our main goal. The jour-
ney of a thousand miles has one more step
to take."

**WRAPPED UP IN HIS WORK: Mark Anderson
creams Drew Brees for a sack, forcing a fumble
in the first quarter.** JIM PRISCHING

**PRAYERFUL POSE:** Linebackers Hunter Hillenmeyer and Brian Urlacher give the signal for a safety after Drew Brees was called for intentional grounding in the end zone. JIM PRISCHING

**HEAVY LIFTING:** Devin Hester raises the George S. Halas Trophy after the Bears' victory. JIM PRISCHING

**POWER COUPLE:** MaryAnne Smith greets husband Lovie after the game. JOHN SMIERCIAK

**FACES OF THE FRANCHISE:** Streamers and confetti obscure Rex Grossman and Brian Urlacher at the trophy presentation. JIM PRISCHING

**FOUNDATION FOUND:** General manager Jerry Angelo's signature moves have been drafting quarterback Rex Grossman and hiring coach Lovie Smith. HEATHER STONE

# JERRY ANGELO

## Franchise architect follows this blueprint to Super Bowl: 'Do it right the first time'

WHEN THE BEARS went into the season with all 22 starters back, it appeared at first that general manager Jerry Angelo wasn't doing enough to improve.

"But that was very important because I liked the team last year," Angelo said. "I liked the intangibles they showed, and I believe you can't have a good football team unless you have a good locker room. We wanted to make sure we kept that as our foundation."

Angelo built the foundation, acquiring every starter except center Olin Kreutz and middle linebacker Brian Urlacher, the two Pro Bowl anchors on offense and defense that Angelo rewarded with big contract extensions. Angelo drafted quarterback Rex Grossman in 2003 and hired coach Lovie Smith in 2004.

"Most people in my position are remembered by their head coach and their quarterback," Angelo said. "If you don't do it right the first time, there isn't a second time."

After spending 14 seasons overseeing scouting for the Tampa Bay Buccaneers, Angelo developed a philosophy of finding defensive linemen first.

"On defense if you have a great front four, it can carry a back end," Angelo said. "You can get better on defense quicker than you can on offense. Until you know what your offense is or isn't, keep feeding the defense. What's the offense? The offense is the quarterback and the line. If you're going to

feed the offense, you feed the line because it allows your quarterback to develop. We want real good receivers, we want a blue-chip running back, but if your line is good and your quarterback is solid, you can manufacture the others."

Angelo helped shepherd the Bucs from perennial losers into winners.

"I'm a specialist in losing," Angelo said when hired after the 2001 draft. "And I know what can help us get out of it. If we stink, it's me."

Angelo's penchant for trading down in the draft and acquiring extra picks has paid off. He got Grossman in 2003 after trading down and got safety Danieal Manning and kick-return specialist Devin Hester after trading down in 2006.

Patience paid off too. After Grossman suffered injuries in his first three seasons, Angelo was criticized for failing to aggressively pursue a dependable backup quarterback. In 2006, he signed veteran Brian Griese, who promptly worked wonders as Grossman stayed healthy for the first time.

Angelo credits the McCaskey ownership and President Ted Phillips for the team's success.

"It all starts at the top," Angelo said. "When you have committed owners and then bring in people at the top who have a plan and are patient, allow people to do their jobs. That's the art of this."

—*Don Pierson*

## BUILDING THE BEARS

Of the 60 players on the Bears roster at season's end (including injured reserve), 54 were signed, traded for or drafted by general manager Jerry Angelo.

About two-thirds of the roster (38 players) arrived since the hiring of Lovie Smith as head coach in 2004.

Here is a breakdown of the 2006 Bears:

### 29
**SIGNED AS FREE AGENTS**

### 3
**WERE ACQUIRED VIA TRADE**

### 28
**WERE DRAFTED BY THE BEARS**

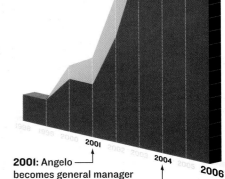

**2001:** Angelo becomes general manager

**2004:** Smith becomes head coach

# LOVIE SMITH

The coach is dignified, direct, respected ... and we'll go from there

WHEN LOVIE SMITH arrived in Chicago, he proclaimed his first priority as coach of the Bears was to beat the Green Bay Packers. He knew how to win friends before he won a game, yet somehow the pronouncement seemed to fall short of the bigger picture.

It turned out to be only a snapshot of what he really had in mind.

"We're a great football team," Smith told the players left over from the 7-9 season of 2003. "You may not believe that, but we're going to be a great football team and go to the Super Bowl."

Smith ends many thoughts with his favorite expression: "And we'll go from there."

One practice at a time, one play at a time, one game at a time, one year at a time, Smith never gets ahead of time. He lives in neither the past nor the future, treating reflection and projection with similar disregard. If he reminisces or dreams, it's mainly to himself.

Complexity is not part of Smith's personality or philosophy. Growing up in Big Sandy, Texas, a name that belies its population of 1,349, Smith learned early the difference between right and wrong. After that, most everything is simple, including the fulfillment of lofty goals.

So it was no surprise to Smith that a team that finished 11-5 in 2005 and had all 22 starters returning might have a good chance to improve. Losing his first home playoff game to Carolina had been a disappointment, but Smith eagerly vowed to "go from there."

"As we went into this season, coming off of last year, we talked about finishing," Smith said. "That was the one part we didn't do at 11-5. So what I'm most proud of is how we finished games. We had a lot of close games, overtime games, and our guys find a way to win. They don't panic, and they expect to win each week."

Panic is what swirled around Smith's quarterback, Rex Grossman, for much of the season.

"Rex is our quarterback, and we'll go from there," Smith said once, twice, three times.

As doubters focused on all kinds of numbers, Smith pointed only to the bottom line-a record of 13-3, good for the No. 1 seed in the NFC.

To Smith, a coach is first and last a teacher. The purpose is to help players reach their potential. Period. Ego trips do not mesh well with Super Bowl trips.

"The personality of our team is we're a bunch of guys who go out and work hard and love the game of football," running back Thomas Jones said.

"He treats us all like men," defensive end Adewale Ogunleye said. "He treats Brian Urlacher the same as a player on the practice squad."

Smith became the first African-American coach to get his team into the Super Bowl. Tony Dungy and the Indianapolis Colts were second.

"I feel blessed to be in that position," Smith said.

Dungy, who brought Smith into the NFL in 1996 as a Tampa Bay Buccaneers assistant, recalls the quality that stood out most was Smith's ability to relate and communicate to different personalities. To both Smith and Dungy, their story is as much about coaching style as color.

"I know the type of person Lovie is," Dungy said. "He has the same Christian convictions I have. He runs his team the same way. I know how those guys are treated in Chicago and how they play-tough, disciplined football without a lot of profanity from coaches or a win-at-all-costs atmosphere."

—*Don Pierson*

**HIGH ON HIS HIRE:** Jerry Angelo brought Smith aboard in 2004. JIM PRISCHING

**THE MANTRA:** "Rex (top) is our quarterback." JIM PRISCHING
**THE TRUTH:** It's no stretch to say the Bears (left) revere their coach. JIM PRISCHING

**TOUCHDOWN IN MIAMI:** Bears players Fred Miller (from left), Rex Grossman, Todd Johnson, John Tait and Brian Griese deboard in South Florida. JIM PRISCHING

# MIAMI

BEARS VS. COLTS AT DOLPHIN STADIUM

*By* DAVID HAUGH

# FINISHED

## BEARS HAND OVER SUPER BOWL TO COLTS

A Chicago kid who grew up loving the Bears makes a play to win a Super Bowl in which they are playing. Sounds like a great story, and it was for Kelvin Hayden. But it hardly created a happy ending for the Bears or their fans.

Hayden's 56-yard interception return for a touchdown with 11 minutes 44 seconds left gave the Indianapolis Colts the decisive score in a 29-17 victory over the Bears in Super Bowl XLI on Feb. 4 at Dolphin Stadium. The Bears had been driving downfield, trailing by five points, when Rex Grossman lofted an ill-advised

pass intended for Muhsin Muhammad that Hayden, inserted only after starter Nick Harper went down with an ankle injury, picked off.

Hayden's heroics took away momentum and any realistic chance the Bears had of winning their first Super Bowl in 21 years.

The Colts used the formula the Bears planned to utilize against them: Establish the run, mix in safe play-action passes and be opportunistic on defense. The Bears' defensive line couldn't stop the Colts' running game, which ground out 191 rushing yards behind a 1-2 running back tandem of Domi-

nic Rhodes and Joseph Addai.

Even more than Super Bowl Most Valuable Player Peyton Manning's efficient 25-for-38 performance for 247 yards with one touchdown and one interception, the running backs permitted the Colts to possess the ball for 38:04. That limited the Bears to

**BROUGHT TO HIS KNEE:**
Rookie Devin Hester, who brought Bears fans to their feet early, watches as the Colts begin their celebration. NUCCIO DI NUZZO

48 offensive plays, eliminated the rhythm of their running game and forced Grossman to feel even more pressure than already existed.

Thomas Jones gained 112 yards on 15 carries, but 52 came on one run, and the ground game never controlled the tempo as everyone at Halas Hall had hoped.

With so few opportunities to make big plays, Grossman resorted to forcing the action in the fourth quarter, when he threw two costly interceptions. Overall, Grossman completed 20 of 28 passes for 165 yards and one touchdown for a passer rating of 68.3.

It was a sloppy game for Grossman and the offense on a rainy night in South Florida. Besides his two interceptions, he lost one fumble on a botched snap and bobbled another that he recovered. Cedric Benson, whose exit with a knee injury late in the first quarter hurt the running game, also fumbled.

Committing five turnovers is no way to win a Super Bowl, not with Manning playing quarterback for the other team. "The turnovers really did us in," coach Lovie Smith said. Everything looked so promising early, when Devin Hester made Super

**IN A FLASH: Devin Hester becomes the first player to return the opening kickoff for a touchdown in Super Bowl history, racing 92 yards.** JIM PRISCHING

**PURPLE RAIN:** The damp weather doesn't stop Rock and Roll Hall of Famer Prince from putting on a dazzling halftime show. SCOTT STRAZZANTE

Bowl history by becoming the first player to return the opening kickoff for a TD with a dazzling 92-yard burst. But on the Colts' second possession, Manning steadied his team by exploiting a breakdown in the secondary for a 53-yard scoring pass to Reggie Wayne.

The Bears had made a minor adjustment by switching cornerback Charles Tillman from the left side to the right, where he would match up more often against Wayne. Stopping the smaller, shiftier Marvin Harrison would be left to Nathan Vasher.

On the touchdown, Tillman passed off Wayne to rookie safety Danieal Manning. But Manning mistakenly was playing man coverage instead of a two-deep zone, where he would have deep responsibility. With Wayne wide open, the Colts' Manning merely had to hit a standing target.

"I think they busted a coverage," Peyton Manning said. In a Super Bowl-or-bust scenario the Bears had outlined for themselves, they took no solace in losing a game in which 30 other teams wanted to play. They came intent on stopping the run, establishing a ground game and limiting mistakes from their quarterback. They did none of those.

"I talked to our team about the steps we have taken in our program over the last three years," Smith said. "We are making progress. We have one more step to go. Last year we had a disappointing loss [against Carolina in the NFC playoffs]. We made progress [in 2006], and I see us doing the same thing [in 2007]. We will be a better ballclub next year than we were this year."

**TAKE YOUR PICK:** Safety Chris Harris corrals a Peyton Manning pass on the Colts' first possession of the game. NUCCIO DI NUZZO

**A LITTLE TOO LATE:** Defensive tackle Tank Johnson gets a hand on Peyton Manning, but not before Manning gets rid of the ball. NUCCIO DI NUZZO

**SMASHING START:** Safety Danieal Manning (38) and linebacker Brian Urlacher put the wraps on Joseph Addai in the first quarter. NUCCIO DI NUZZO

**DOWN AND DIRTY: Rex Grossman falls to the ground in the third quarter of Super Bowl XLI. Grossman was sacked once and threw two interceptions. SCOTT STRAZZANTE**

**NO, YOU DON'T: Bears tight end Desmond Clark turns defender, breaking up a pass as the Colts' Jason David (42) and Antoine Bethea go for the interception.** SCOTT STRAZZANTE

**LANDING GEAR: Bears running back Thomas Jones is tackled by the Colts' Antoine Bethea in the fourth quarter. Jones rushed for 112 yards.** NUCCIO DI NUZZO

**SQUEEZE PLAY:** Bears linebacker Lance Briggs puts the clamps on Colts rookie running back Joseph Addai. Briggs led the Bears with 11 solo tackles in the Super Bowl. JIM PRISCHING

**FLINGIN' IN THE RAIN:** Rex Grossman gets set to pull the trigger on a pass in the fourth quarter. He completed 20 of 28 passes for 165 yards and a touchdown. NUCCIO DI NUZZO

★ **SUPER BOWL XLI** • AT DOLPHIN STADIUM ★

| | | | | | |
|---|---|---|---|---|---|
| **COLTS** | 6 | 10 | 6 | 7 | **29** |
| **BEARS** | 14 | 0 | 3 | 0 | **17** |

## DRIVES

### FIRST HALF

| | START | PLAYS | YDS. | RESULT |
|---|---|---|---|---|
| CHI | — | — | — | Touchdown |
| IND | IND 30 | 5 | 11 | Interception |
| CHI | CHI 35 | 3 | 7 | Punt |
| IND | IND 20 | 9 | 80 | Touchdown |
| CHI | — | — | — | Fumble |
| IND | CHI 34 | 1 | -7 | Fumble |
| CHI | CHI 43 | 4 | 57 | Touchdown |
| IND | IND 16 | 3 | 3 | Punt |
| CHI | CHI 35 | 2 | 8 | Fumble |
| IND | CHI 43 | 3 | 7 | Punt |
| CHI | CHI 5 | 3 | 8 | Punt |
| IND | IND 42 | 8 | 47 | Field goal |
| CHI | CHI 22 | 3 | 6 | Punt |
| IND | IND 42 | 7 | 58 | Touchdown |
| CHI | CHI 36 | 3 | 9 | Punt |
| IND | IND 35 | 7 | 28 | Fumble |
| CHI | CHI 36 | 1 | -1 | Fumble |
| IND | CHI 35 | 5 | 18 | Missed FG |

### SECOND HALF

| | START | PLAYS | YDS. | RESULT |
|---|---|---|---|---|
| IND | IND 38 | 13 | 56 | Field goal |
| CHI | CHI 32 | 4 | 1 | Punt |
| IND | IND 36 | 6 | 62 | Field goal |
| CHI | IND 40 | 6 | 14 | Field goal |
| IND | IND 32 | 6 | 18 | Punt |
| CHI | CHI 20 | 3 | 18 | Interception |
| CHI | CHI 20 | 4 | 19 | Interception |
| IND | CHI 41 | 4 | 1 | Punt |
| CHI | CHI 8 | 8 | 39 | Downs |
| IND | CHI 47 | 8 | 31 | Downs |
| CHI | CHI 16 | 5 | 48 | End of game |

## SCORING

### FIRST QUARTER

**BEARS:** Hester 92 kickoff return (Gould kick), 14:46
**COLTS:** Wayne 53 pass from Manning (kick aborted), 6:50
**BEARS:** Muhammad 4 pass from Grossman (Gould kick), 4:34

### SECOND QUARTER

**COLTS:** Vinatieri 29 FG, 11:17
**COLTS:** Rhodes 1 run (Vinatieri kick), 6:09

### THIRD QUARTER

**COLTS:** Vinatieri 24 FG, 7:26
**COLTS:** Vinatieri 20 FG, 3:16
**BEARS:** Gould 44 FG, 1:14

### FOURTH QUARTER

**COLTS:** Hayden 56 interception return (Vinatieri kick), 11:44

## TEAM STATS

| CATEGORY | IND | CHI |
|---|---|---|
| First downs | 24 | 11 |
| (Rush-pass-penalty) | 12-11-1 | 3-8-0 |
| Third downs | 8-18 | 3-10 |
| Fourth downs | 0-1 | 0-1 |
| Total net yards | 430 | 265 |
| Rushes-yards | 42-191 | 19-111 |
| Passing yards | 239 | 154 |
| Att.-comp.-int. | 38-25-1 | 28-20-2 |
| Sacked-yards lost | 1-8 | 1-11 |
| Kick returns-yards | 4-89 | 6-138 |
| Punt returns-yards | 3-42 | 1-3 |
| Punts-average | 4-40.5 | 5-45.2 |
| Fumbles-lost | 2-2 | 4-3 |
| Penalties-yards | 6-40 | 4-35 |
| Possession | 38:04 | 21:56 |

## INDIVIDUAL STATS

### PASSING

| COLTS | ATT. | COMP. | YDS. | TD | INT. | BEARS | ATT. | COMP. | YDS. | TD | INT. |
|---|---|---|---|---|---|---|---|---|---|---|---|
| Manning | 38 | 25 | 247 | 1 | 1 | Grossman | 28 | 20 | 165 | 1 | 2 |

### RUSHING

| COLTS | NO. | YDS. | AVG. | LNG. | TD | BEARS | NO. | YDS. | AVG. | LNG. | TD |
|---|---|---|---|---|---|---|---|---|---|---|---|
| Rhodes | 21 | 113 | 5.4 | 36 | 1 | Jones | 15 | 112 | 7.5 | 52 | 0 |
| Addai | 19 | 77 | 4.1 | 14 | 0 | Grossman | 2 | 0 | 0.0 | 0 | 0 |
| Clark | 1 | 1 | 1.0 | 1 | 0 | Benson | 2 | -1 | -0.5 | 4 | 0 |
| Manning | 1 | 0 | 0.0 | 0 | 0 | | | | | | |

### RECEIVING

| COLTS | NO. | YDS. | AVG. | LNG. | TD | BEARS | NO. | YDS. | AVG. | LNG. | TD |
|---|---|---|---|---|---|---|---|---|---|---|---|
| Addai | 10 | 66 | 6.6 | 12 | 0 | Clark | 6 | 64 | 10.7 | 18 | 0 |
| Harrison | 5 | 59 | 11.8 | 22 | 0 | Berrian | 4 | 38 | 9.5 | 14 | 0 |
| Clark | 4 | 36 | 9.0 | 17 | 0 | Jones | 4 | 18 | 4.5 | 14 | 0 |
| Wayne | 2 | 61 | 30.5 | 53 | 1 | Muhammad | 3 | 35 | 11.7 | 22 | 1 |
| Fletcher | 2 | 9 | 4.5 | 6 | 0 | McKie | 2 | 8 | 4.0 | 4 | 0 |
| Rhodes | 1 | 8 | 8.0 | 8 | 0 | Davis | 1 | 2 | 2.0 | 2 | 0 |
| Utecht | 1 | 8 | 8.0 | 8 | 0 | | | | | | |

### INTERCEPTIONS (NO.-RETURN YARDS)

**COLTS:** Hayden (1-56), Sanders (1-38)      **BEARS:** C. Harris (1-6)

### FUMBLES LOST

**COLTS:** Fletcher, Manning      **BEARS:** Grossman, Benson, Reid

**TIME:** 3:31 • **PAID ATTENDANCE:** 74,512

**BIRD'S-EYE VIEW: It's tempting to say this CBS cameraman has the best seat in Soldier Field, but he has no place to sit down.** E. JASON WAMBSGANS

# 2006 CHICAGO BEARS ROSTER

## ACTIVE ROSTER

●● PLAYED FOR BEARS  ○ PLAYED FOR OTHER NFL TEAM

| NO. | PLAYER | POS. | COLLEGE | HT. | WT. | NFL CAREER | HOW ACQUIRED |
|---|---|---|---|---|---|---|---|
| 97 | Mark Anderson | DE | Alabama | 6-4 | 255 | 06 | Fifth-round draft pick, 2006 |
| 94 | Brendon Ayanbadejo | LB | UCLA | 6-1 | 228 | 05 06 | Traded from Dolphins, 2005 |
| 32 | Cedric Benson | RB | Texas | 5-11 | 220 | 05 06 | First-round draft pick, 2005 |
| 80 | Bernard Berrian | WR | Fresno State | 6-1 | 185 | 04 05 06 | Third-round draft pick, 2004 |
| 70 | Alfonso Boone | DT | Mt. San Antonio JC | 6-4 | 318 | 00 01 02 03 04 05 06 | Signed off Lions' practice squad, 2000 |
| 16 | Mark Bradley | WR | Oklahoma | 6-2 | 198 | 05 06 | Second-round draft pick, 2005 |
| 55 | Lance Briggs | LB | Arizona | 6-1 | 240 | 03 04 05 06 | Third-round draft pick, 2003 |
| 96 | Alex Brown | DE | Florida | 6-3 | 260 | 02 03 04 05 06 | Fourth-round draft pick, 2002 |
| 74 | Ruben Brown | G | Pittsburgh | 6-3 | 300 | 04 05 06 | Signed as free agent, 2004 |
| 88 | Desmond Clark | TE | Wake Forest | 6-3 | 249 | 03 04 05 06 | Signed as free agent, 2003 |
| 81 | Rashied Davis | WR | San Jose State | 5-9 | 183 | 05 06 | Signed as free agent, 2005 |
| 22 | Tyler Everett | SS | Ohio State | 5-11 | 202 | 06 | Signed as free agent, 2006 |
| 12 | Justin Gage | WR | Missouri | 6-4 | 212 | 03 04 05 06 | Fifth-round draft pick, 2003 |
| 90 | Antonio Garay | DT | Boston College | 6-4 | 303 | 05 06 | Signed as free agent, 2005 |
| 63 | Roberto Garza | G | Texas A&M-Kingsville | 6-2 | 305 | 05 06 | Signed as free agent, 2005 |
| 85 | John Gilmore | TE | Penn State | 6-5 | 257 | 02 03 04 05 06 | Signed as free agent, 2002 |
| 9 | Robbie Gould | K | Penn State | 6-0 | 183 | 05 06 | Signed as free agent, 2005 |
| 14 | Brian Griese | QB | Michigan | 6-3 | 214 | 06 | Signed as free agent, 2006 |
| 8 | Rex Grossman | QB | Florida | 6-1 | 217 | 03 04 05 06 | First-round draft pick, 2003 |
| 46 | Chris Harris | FS | Louisiana-Monroe | 6-0 | 205 | 05 06 | Sixth-round draft pick, 2005 |
| 23 | Devin Hester | CB | Miami | 5-11 | 186 | 06 | Second-round draft pick, 2006 |
| 92 | Hunter Hillenmeyer | LB | Vanderbilt | 6-4 | 238 | 03 04 05 06 | Signed as free agent, 2003 |
| 71 | Israel Idonije | DT | Manitoba | 6-6 | 270 | 04 05 06 | Signed as free agent, 2004 |
| 53 | Leon Joe | LB | Maryland | 6-1 | 230 | 05 06 | Claimed off waivers from Cardinals, 2005 |
| 99 | Tank Johnson | NT | Washington | 6-3 | 300 | 04 05 06 | Second-round draft pick, 2004 |
| 35 | Todd Johnson | SS | Florida | 6-1 | 200 | 03 04 05 06 | Fourth-round draft pick, 2003 |
| 20 | Thomas Jones | RB | Virginia | 5-10 | 215 | 04 05 06 | Signed as free agent, 2004 |
| 57 | Olin Kreutz | C | Washington | 6-2 | 292 | 98 99 00 01 02 03 04 05 06 | Third-round draft pick, 1998 |
| 65 | Patrick Mannelly | LS | Duke | 6-5 | 265 | 98 99 00 01 02 03 04 05 06 | Sixth-round draft pick, 1998 |
| 38 | Danieal Manning | FS | Abilene Christian | 5-11 | 196 | 06 | Second-round draft pick, 2006 |
| 24 | Ricky Manning Jr. | CB | UCLA | 5-9 | 188 | 06 | Signed as free agent, 2006 |
| 4 | Brad Maynard | P | Ball State | 6-1 | 186 | 01 02 03 04 05 06 | Signed as free agent, 2001 |
| 58 | Darrell McClover | LB | Miami | 6-2 | 226 | 06 | Signed as free agent, 2006 |
| 37 | Jason McKie | FB | Temple | 5-11 | 243 | 03 04 05 06 | Signed as free agent, 2003 |
| 60 | Terrence Metcalf | G | Mississippi | 6-3 | 318 | 02 03 04 05 06 | Third-round draft pick, 2002 |
| 69 | Fred Miller | T | Baylor | 6-7 | 314 | 05 06 | Signed as free agent, 2005 |
| 87 | Muhsin Muhammad | WR | Michigan State | 6-2 | 215 | 05 06 | Signed as free agent, 2005 |
| 68 | Anthony Oakley | G/C | Western Kentucky | 6-4 | 298 | 05 06 | Signed as free agent, 2005 |
| 93 | Adewale Ogunleye | DE | Indiana | 6-4 | 260 | 04 05 06 | Traded from Dolphins, 2004 |
| 18 | Kyle Orton | QB | Purdue | 6-4 | 217 | 05 06 | Fourth-round draft pick, 2005 |
| 29 | Adrian Peterson | RB | Georgia Southern | 5-10 | 210 | 02 03 04 05 06 | Sixth-round draft pick, 2002 |
| 82 | Gabe Reid | TE | Brigham Young | 6-3 | 252 | 03 04 05 06 | Claimed off Titans' practice squad, 2003 |
| 48 | J.D. Runnels | FB | Oklahoma | 5-11 | 240 | 06 | Sixth-round draft pick, 2002 |
| 95 | Ian Scott | NT | Florida | 6-3 | 302 | 03 04 05 06 | Fourth-round draft pick, 2003 |
| 78 | John St. Clair | T | Virginia | 6-5 | 315 | 05 06 | Signed as free agent, 2005 |
| 76 | John Tait | T | Brigham Young | 6-6 | 312 | 04 05 06 | Signed as free agent, 2004 |
| 33 | Charles Tillman | CB | Louisiana-Lafayette | 6-1 | 196 | 03 04 05 06 | Second-round draft pick, 2003 |
| 27 | Nick Turnbull | S | Florida International | 6-2 | 222 | 06 | Claimed off waivers from Falcons, 2006 |
| 54 | Brian Urlacher | LB | New Mexico | 6-4 | 258 | 00 01 02 03 04 05 06 | First-round draft pick, 2000 |
| 31 | Nathan Vasher | CB | Texas | 5-10 | 180 | 04 05 06 | Fourth-round draft pick, 2004 |
| 21 | Dante Wesley | CB | Arkansas-Pine Bluff | 6-1 | 210 | 06 | Signed as free agent, 2006 |
| 59 | Rod Wilson | LB | South Carolina | 6-2 | 230 | 05 06 | Seventh-round draft pick, 2005 |
| 44 | Cameron Worrell | SS | Fresno State | 5-11 | 194 | 03 04 05 06 | Signed as free agent, 2003 |

## INJURED RESERVE

| NO. | PLAYER | POS. | COLLEGE | HT. | WT. | NFL CAREER | HOW ACQUIRED |
|---|---|---|---|---|---|---|---|
| 30 | Mike Brown | SS | Nebraska | 5-10 | 207 | 00 01 02 03 04 05 06 | Second-round draft pick, 2000 |
| 17 | Airese Currie | WR | Clemson | 5-11 | 185 | 05 06 | Fifth-round draft pick, 2005 |
| 98 | Dusty Dvoracek | NT | Oklahoma | 6-3 | 305 | 06 | Third-round draft pick, 2006 |
| 91 | Tommie Harris | DT | Oklahoma | 6-3 | 295 | 04 05 06 | First-round draft pick, 2004 |
| 47 | Bryan Johnson | FB | Boise State | 6-1 | 244 | 04 05 06 | Traded from Redskins, 2004 |
| 36 | Brandon McGowan | SS | Maine | 5-11 | 205 | 05 06 | Signed as free agent, 2005 |
| 52 | Jamar Williams | LB | Arizona State | 6-0 | 234 | 06 | Signed as free agent, 2006 |

PRACTICE SQUAD: 86 Richard Angulo (TE), 72 Bryan Copeland (DE), 83 Mike Hass (WR), 75 Mark LeVoir (T), 64 Tyler Reed (G), 84 Brandon Rideau (WR), 45 Dwayne Slay (LB)

**REX'S REGIMENT:** The offense gathers around Rex Grossman during the **NFC** semifinal victory. NUCCIO DI NUZZO

# REGULAR-SEASON STATISTICAL SUMMARY

## FINAL STANDINGS

| NFC NORTH | W | L | PF | PA |
|---|---|---|---|---|
| *yz-BEARS | 13 | 3 | 427 | 255 |
| Green Bay | 8 | 8 | 301 | 366 |
| Minnesota | 6 | 10 | 282 | 327 |
| Detroit | 3 | 13 | 305 | 398 |

| NFC EAST | W | L | PF | PA |
|---|---|---|---|---|
| y-Philadelphia | 10 | 6 | 398 | 328 |
| x-Dallas | 9 | 7 | 425 | 350 |
| x-N.Y. Giants | 8 | 8 | 355 | 362 |
| Washington | 5 | 11 | 307 | 376 |

| NFC SOUTH | W | L | PF | PA |
|---|---|---|---|---|
| yz-New Orleans | 10 | 6 | 413 | 322 |
| Carolina | 8 | 8 | 270 | 305 |
| Atlanta | 7 | 9 | 292 | 328 |
| Tampa Bay | 4 | 12 | 211 | 353 |

| NFC WEST | W | L | PF | PA |
|---|---|---|---|---|
| y-Seattle | 9 | 7 | 335 | 341 |
| St. Louis | 8 | 8 | 367 | 381 |
| San Francisco | 7 | 9 | 298 | 412 |
| Arizona | 5 | 11 | 314 | 389 |

| AFC NORTH | W | L | PF | PA |
|---|---|---|---|---|
| yz-Baltimore | 13 | 3 | 353 | 201 |
| Cincinnati | 8 | 8 | 373 | 331 |
| Pittsburgh | 8 | 8 | 353 | 315 |
| Cleveland | 4 | 12 | 238 | 356 |

| AFC EAST | W | L | PF | PA |
|---|---|---|---|---|
| y-New England | 12 | 4 | 385 | 237 |
| x-N.Y. Jets | 10 | 6 | 316 | 295 |
| Buffalo | 7 | 9 | 300 | 311 |
| Miami | 6 | 10 | 260 | 283 |

| AFC SOUTH | W | L | PF | PA |
|---|---|---|---|---|
| y-Indianapolis | 12 | 4 | 427 | 360 |
| Tennessee | 8 | 8 | 324 | 400 |
| Jacksonville | 8 | 8 | 371 | 274 |
| Houston | 6 | 10 | 267 | 366 |

| AFC WEST | W | L | PF | PA |
|---|---|---|---|---|
| *yz-San Diego | 14 | 2 | 492 | 303 |
| x-Kansas City | 9 | 7 | 331 | 315 |
| Denver | 9 | 7 | 319 | 305 |
| Oakland | 2 | 14 | 168 | 332 |

x-wild-card team   y-division winner   z-clinched first-round bye   *-clinched home-field advantage

## SCORING BY QUARTER

| | | | | | | |
|---|---|---|---|---|---|---|
| BEARS | 73 | 140 | 101 | 110 | 3 | **427** |
| OPPONENTS | 47 | 71 | 48 | 89 | 0 | **255** |

## TEAM STATS

| CATEGORY | BEARS | OPPONENTS |
|---|---|---|
| First downs | 300 | 258 |
| By rushing | 103 | 77 |
| By passing | 161 | 159 |
| By penalty | 36 | 22 |
| Third downs | 85-231 | 74-239 |
| Third-down efficiency | 36.8% | 31.0% |
| Fourth downs | 9-13 | 10-16 |
| Fourth-down efficiency | 69.2% | 62.5% |
| Total net yards | 5,199 | 4,706 |
| Yards per game | 324.9 | 294.1 |
| Total plays | 1,042 | 1,023 |
| Yards per play | 5.0 | 4.6 |
| Total yards rushing | 1,918 | 1,590 |
| Rushing attempts | 503 | 402 |
| Rushing yards per game | 119.9 | 99.4 |
| Net yards passing | 3,281 | 3,116 |
| Passing yards per game | 205.1 | 194.8 |
| Attempted-completed | 514-282 | 581-328 |
| Completion percentage | 54.9% | 56.5% |
| Had intercepted | 22 | 24 |
| Sacked-yards lost | 25-165 | 40-272 |
| Punts-average | 77-44.2 | 100-43.7 |
| Net punting average | 37.6 | 35.2 |
| Fumbles-lost | 26-14 | 32-20 |
| Penalties-yards | 112-923 | 132-1,084 |
| Touchdowns | 47 | 29 |
| By rushing | 14 | 7 |
| By passing | 24 | 18 |
| By return | 9 | 4 |
| Possession average | 30:34 | 29:26 |

## NFL RANK

| | |
|---|---|
| Total offense | 15th |
| Pass offense | 14th |
| Rush offense | 15th |
| Scoring offense | 2nd (tie) |
| Total defense | 5th |
| Pass defense | 11th |
| Rush defense | 6th |
| Scoring defense | 3rd |

## INDIVIDUAL STATS

### PASSING

| PASSING | ATT. | COMP. | YARDS | COMP.% | YDS./ATT. | TD | TD% | INT. | INT.% | LNG. | SACKED-YDS. | RATING |
|---|---|---|---|---|---|---|---|---|---|---|---|---|
| Rex Grossman | 480 | 262 | 3,193 | 54.6 | 6.7 | 23 | 4.8 | 20 | 4.2 | 62 | 21-142 | 73.9 |
| Brian Griese | 32 | 18 | 220 | 56.3 | 6.9 | 1 | 3.1 | 2 | 6.2 | 75 | 3-22 | 62.0 |
| Brad Maynard | 1 | 1 | 37 | 100.0 | 37.0 | 0 | 0.0 | 0 | 0.0 | 37 | 0-0 | 118.8 |
| Thomas Jones | 1 | 1 | -4 | 100.0 | -4.0 | 0 | 0.0 | 0 | 0.0 | -4 | 1-1 | 79.2 |
| **BEARS** | 514 | 282 | 3,446 | 54.9 | 6.7 | 24 | 4.7 | 22 | 4.3 | 75 | 25-165 | 73.5 |
| **OPPONENTS** | 581 | 328 | 3,388 | 56.5 | 5.8 | 18 | 3.1 | 24 | 4.1 | 64 | 40-272 | 66.5 |

### RUSHING

| RUSHING | NO. | YARDS | AVG. | LNG. | TD |
|---|---|---|---|---|---|
| Thomas Jones | 296 | 1,210 | 4.1 | 30 | 6 |
| Cedric Benson | 157 | 647 | 4.1 | 30 | 6 |
| Adrian Peterson | 10 | 41 | 4.1 | 11 | 2 |
| Jason McKie | 8 | 18 | 2.3 | 7 | 0 |
| Bernard Berrian | 2 | 5 | 2.5 | 5 | 0 |
| Rex Grossman | 24 | 2 | 0.1 | 22 | 0 |
| Brian Griese | 6 | -5 | -0.8 | 0 | 0 |
| **BEARS** | 503 | 1,918 | 3.8 | 30 | 14 |
| **OPPONENTS** | 402 | 1,590 | 4.0 | 53 | 7 |

### RECEIVING

| RECEIVING | NO. | YARDS | AVG. | LNG. | TD |
|---|---|---|---|---|---|
| Muhsin Muhammad | 60 | 863 | 14.4 | 40 | 5 |
| Bernard Berrian | 51 | 775 | 15.2 | 62 | 6 |
| Desmond Clark | 45 | 626 | 13.9 | 33 | 6 |
| Rashied Davis | 22 | 303 | 13.8 | 31 | 0 |
| Mark Bradley | 14 | 282 | 20.1 | 75 | 3 |
| Jason McKie | 25 | 162 | 6.5 | 26 | 0 |
| Thomas Jones | 36 | 154 | 4.3 | 21 | 0 |
| Adrian Peterson | 6 | 88 | 14.7 | 37 | 0 |
| Justin Gage | 4 | 68 | 17.0 | 34 | 0 |
| Cedric Benson | 8 | 54 | 6.8 | 22 | 0 |
| John Gilmore | 6 | 38 | 6.3 | 18 | 2 |
| Gabe Reid | 4 | 37 | 9.3 | 19 | 0 |
| Rex Grossman | 1 | -4 | -4.0 | -4 | 0 |
| **BEARS** | 282 | 3,446 | 12.2 | 75 | 24 |
| **OPPONENTS** | 328 | 3,388 | 10.3 | 64 | 18 |

### KICK RETURNS

| KICK RETURNS | NO. | YARDS | AVG. | LNG. | TD |
|---|---|---|---|---|---|
| Rashied Davis | 32 | 753 | 23.5 | 42 | 0 |
| Devin Hester | 20 | 528 | 26.4 | 96 | 2 |
| Adrian Peterson | 3 | 49 | 16.3 | 25 | 0 |
| Danieal Manning | 1 | 20 | 20.0 | 20 | 0 |
| Jason McKie | 1 | 11 | 11.0 | 11 | 0 |
| Darrell McClover | 1 | 9 | 9.0 | 9 | 0 |
| Muhsin Muhammad | 1 | 3 | 3.0 | 3 | 0 |
| **BEARS** | 59 | 1,373 | 23.3 | 96 | 2 |
| **OPPONENTS** | 83 | 1,730 | 20.8 | 35 | 0 |

### PUNT RETURNS

| PUNT RETURNS | NO. | F.C. | YARDS | AVG. | LNG. | TD |
|---|---|---|---|---|---|---|
| Devin Hester | 47 | 12 | 600 | 12.8 | 84 | 3 |
| Bernard Berrian | 2 | 0 | 7 | 3.5 | 7 | 0 |
| Dante Wesley | 1 | 0 | 0 | 0 | 0 | 0 |
| **BEARS** | 50 | 12 | 607 | 12.1 | 84 | 3 |
| **OPPONENTS** | 38 | 14 | 367 | 9.7 | 48 | 0 |

### SCORING

| SCORING | TDR | TDP | TDRT | PAT | FG | S | PTS. |
|---|---|---|---|---|---|---|---|
| Robbie Gould | 0 | 0 | 0 | 47/47 | 32/36 | 0 | 143 |
| Cedric Benson | 6 | 0 | 0 | 0 | 0 | 0 | 36 |
| Bernard Berrian | 0 | 6 | 0 | 0 | 0 | 0 | 36 |
| Desmond Clark | 0 | 6 | 0 | 0 | 0 | 0 | 36 |
| Devin Hester | 0 | 0 | 6 | 0 | 0 | 0 | 36 |
| Thomas Jones | 6 | 0 | 0 | 0 | 0 | 0 | 36 |
| Muhsin Muhammad | 0 | 5 | 0 | 0 | 0 | 0 | 30 |
| Mark Bradley | 0 | 3 | 0 | 0 | 0 | 0 | 18 |
| Rashied Davis | 0 | 2 | 0 | 0 | 0 | 0 | 12 |
| John Gilmore | 0 | 2 | 0 | 0 | 0 | 0 | 12 |
| Adrian Peterson | 2 | 0 | 0 | 0 | 0 | 0 | 12 |
| Mike Brown | 0 | 0 | 1 | 0 | 0 | 0 | 6 |
| Ricky Manning Jr. | 0 | 0 | 1 | 0 | 0 | 0 | 6 |
| Charles Tillman | 0 | 0 | 1 | 0 | 0 | 0 | 6 |
| Tank Johnson | 0 | 0 | 0 | 0 | 0 | 1 | 2 |
| **BEARS** | 14 | 24 | 9 | 47/47 | 32/36 | 1 | 427 |
| **OPPONENTS** | 7 | 18 | 4 | 27/28 | 18/27 | 0 | 255 |

### FIELD GOALS

| FIELD GOALS | 10-19 | 20-29 | 30-39 | 40-49 | 50+ |
|---|---|---|---|---|---|
| Robbie Gould | 0-0 | 6-6 | 14-16 | 12-14 | 0-0 |
| OPPONENTS | 0-0 | 9-9 | 2-5 | 6-9 | 1-4 |

### PUNTING

| PUNTING | NO. | AVG. | NET | TB | IN 20 | LNG. | BLK. |
|---|---|---|---|---|---|---|---|
| Brad Maynard | 77 | 44.2 | 37.6 | 7 | 24 | 65 | 0 |
| OPPONENTS | 100 | 43.7 | 35.2 | 12 | 23 | 67 | 0 |

### INTERCEPTIONS

| INTERCEPTIONS | NO. | YARDS | AVG. | LNG. | TD |
|---|---|---|---|---|---|
| Ricky Manning Jr. | 5 | 113 | 22.6 | 54 | 1 |
| Charles Tillman | 5 | 32 | 6.4 | 13 | 0 |
| Nathan Vasher | 3 | 11 | 3.7 | 7 | 0 |
| Brian Urlacher | 3 | 38 | 12.7 | 36 | 0 |
| Lance Briggs | 2 | 18 | 9.0 | 18 | 0 |
| Alex Brown | 2 | 22 | 11.0 | 18 | 0 |
| Chris Harris | 2 | 19 | 9.5 | 16 | 0 |
| Danieal Manning | 2 | 26 | 13.0 | 15 | 0 |
| **BEARS** | 24 | 279 | 11.6 | 54 | 1 |
| **OPPONENTS** | 22 | 321 | 14.6 | 55 | 4 |

### SACKS

| SACKS | NO. |
|---|---|
| Anderson | 12.0 |
| A. Brown | 7.0 |
| Ogunleye | 6.5 |
| T. Harris | 5.0 |
| Ta. Johnson | 3.5 |
| Boone | 2.0 |
| R. Manning | 2.0 |
| Briggs | 1.0 |
| Worrell | 1.0 |
| **BEARS** | 40.0 |
| **OPPONENTS** | 25.0 |

### TACKLES*

| TACKLES* | NO. | SOLO | ASST. |
|---|---|---|---|
| Brian Urlacher | 185 | 93 | 92 |
| Lance Briggs | 176 | 117 | 59 |
| Charles Tillman | 88 | 67 | 21 |
| Danieal Manning | 80 | 46 | 34 |
| Alex Brown | 71 | 44 | 27 |
| Hunter Hillenmeyer | 68 | 32 | 36 |
| Adewale Ogunleye | 58 | 34 | 24 |
| Ricky Manning Jr. | 55 | 41 | 14 |
| Chris Harris | 54 | 42 | 12 |
| Mark Anderson | 48 | 35 | 13 |
| Tommie Harris | 48 | 30 | 18 |

*Tackles are not an official NFL statistic; leaders shown only.

## ABBREVIATIONS

**ATT.** Pass attempts
**COMP.** Pass completions
**COMP.%** Completion percentage

**YDS./ATT.** Yards per pass attempt
**TD** Touchdowns
**TD%** Touchdown percentage
**INT.** Interceptions
**INT.%** Interception percentage

**NO.** Number
**AVG.** Average
**F.C.** Fair catches
**TDR** Rushing touchdowns
**TDP** Passing touchdowns

**TDRT:** Return touchdowns
**PAT** Points after touchdown
**FG** Field goals
**S** Safeties
**PTS.** Points scored

**TB** Touchbacks
**IN 20** Punts inside opponent's 20
**BLK.** Blocked punts
**ASST.** Assists

## GAME 1 • SEPT. 10 AT LAMBEAU FIELD

| | | | | | |
|---|---|---|---|---|---|
| **BEARS** | 7 | 9 | 3 | 7 | **26** |
| **PACKERS** | 0 | 0 | 0 | 0 | **0** |

### SCORING
**FIRST QUARTER**
**BEARS:** Berrian 49 pass from Grossman (Gould kick), 12:05

**SECOND QUARTER**
**BEARS:** Gould 40 FG, 13:44
**BEARS:** Gould 39 FG, 6:29
**BEARS:** Gould 28 FG, 4:38

**THIRD QUARTER**
**BEARS:** Gould 30 FG, 1:47

**FOURTH QUARTER**
**BEARS:** Hester 84 punt return (Gould kick), 14:06

### TEAM STATS

| CATEGORY | CHI | GB |
|---|---|---|
| First downs | 18 | 14 |
| (Rush-pass-penalty) | 4-12-2 | 6-8-0 |
| Third downs | 4-14 | 1-11 |
| Fourth downs | 1-1 | 2-3 |
| Total net yards | 361 | 267 |
| Rushes-yards | 36-109 | 23-103 |
| Passing yards | 252 | 164 |
| Att.-comp.-int. | 27-19-1 | 30-16-2 |
| Sacked-yards lost | 1-6 | 3-22 |
| Kick returns-yards | 1-18 | 7-129 |
| Punt returns-yards | 5-104 | 3-44 |
| Punts-average | 4-47.3 | 6-45.0 |
| Fumbles-lost | 0-0 | 1-1 |
| Penalties-yards | 4-25 | 5-45 |
| Possession | 34:05 | 25:55 |

### INDIVIDUAL LEADERS

| PASSING | ATT. | COMP. | YDS. | TD | INT. |
|---|---|---|---|---|---|
| **CHI:** Grossman | 26 | 18 | 262 | 1 | 1 |
| Jones | 1 | 1 | -4 | 0 | 0 |
| **GB:** Favre | 29 | 15 | 170 | 0 | 2 |
| Ryan | 1 | 1 | 16 | 0 | 0 |

| RUSHING | NO. | YDS. | AVG. | LNG. | TD |
|---|---|---|---|---|---|
| **CHI:** Jones | 21 | 63 | 3.0 | 17 | 0 |
| Benson | 11 | 34 | 3.1 | 7 | 0 |
| McKie | 3 | 10 | 3.3 | 6 | 0 |
| Grossman | 1 | 2 | 2.0 | 2 | 0 |
| **GB:** Green | 20 | 110 | 5.5 | 14 | 0 |
| Favre | 1 | 0 | 0.0 | 0 | 0 |
| Gado | 2 | -7 | -3.5 | -3 | 0 |

| RECEIVING | NO. | YDS. | AVG. | LNG. | TD |
|---|---|---|---|---|---|
| **CHI:** Muhammad | 6 | 102 | 17.0 | 27 | 0 |
| Clark | 5 | 77 | 15.4 | 33 | 0 |
| McKie | 4 | 26 | 6.5 | 10 | 0 |
| Berrian | 1 | 49 | 49.0 | 49 | 1 |
| Davis | 1 | 8 | 8.0 | 8 | 0 |
| Jones | 1 | 0 | 0.0 | 0 | 0 |
| Grossman | 1 | -4 | -4.0 | -4 | 0 |
| **GB:** Driver | 7 | 96 | 13.7 | 24 | 0 |
| Green | 3 | 22 | 7.3 | 13 | 0 |
| Ferguson | 2 | 17 | 8.5 | 10 | 0 |
| Lee | 1 | 25 | 25.0 | 25 | 0 |
| Herron | 1 | 16 | 16.0 | 16 | 0 |
| Gado | 1 | 5 | 5.0 | 5 | 0 |
| Jennings | 1 | 5 | 5.0 | 5 | 0 |

**INTERCEPTIONS** (NO.-RETURN YARDS)
**CHI:** D. Manning (1-15), Tillman (1-13)
**GB:** Barnett (1-0)

**FUMBLES LOST**
**GB:** Herron

**TIME:** 2:53 • **PAID ATTENDANCE:** 70,918

---

## GAME 2 • SEPT. 17 AT SOLDIER FIELD

| | | | | | |
|---|---|---|---|---|---|
| **LIONS** | 0 | 0 | 7 | 0 | **7** |
| **BEARS** | 10 | 14 | 7 | 3 | **34** |

### SCORING
**FIRST QUARTER**
**BEARS:** Gilmore 3 pass from Grossman (Gould kick), 10:11
**BEARS:** Gould 32 FG, 6:19

**SECOND QUARTER**
**BEARS:** Berrian 41 pass from Grossman (Gould kick), 14:16
**BEARS:** Clark 31 pass from Grossman (Gould kick), 3:36

**THIRD QUARTER**
**LIONS:** Kitna 1 run (Hanson kick), 10:20
**BEARS:** Gilmore 5 pass from Grossman (Gould kick), 0:32

**FOURTH QUARTER**
**BEARS:** Gould 45 FG, 10:03

### TEAM STATS

| CATEGORY | DET | CHI |
|---|---|---|
| First downs | 15 | 22 |
| (Rush-pass-penalty) | 2-11-2 | 4-16-2 |
| Third downs | 1-9 | 6-12 |
| Fourth downs | 1-1 | 0-0 |
| Total net yards | 245 | 383 |
| Rushes-yards | 14-46 | 34-89 |
| Passing yards | 199 | 294 |
| Att.-comp.-int. | 30-23-0 | 28-21-0 |
| Sacked-yards lost | 6-31 | 0-0 |
| Kick returns-yards | 4-66 | 2-39 |
| Punt returns-yards | 1-5 | 4-21 |
| Punts-average | 6-43.0 | 3-44.3 |
| Fumbles-lost | 3-3 | 2-1 |
| Penalties-yards | 14-104 | 6-93 |
| Possession | 27:00 | 33:00 |

### INDIVIDUAL LEADERS

| PASSING | ATT. | COMP. | YDS. | TD | INT. |
|---|---|---|---|---|---|
| **DET:** Kitna | 30 | 23 | 230 | 0 | 0 |
| **CHI:** Grossman | 27 | 20 | 289 | 4 | 0 |
| Griese | 1 | 1 | 5 | 0 | 0 |

| RUSHING | NO. | YDS. | AVG. | LNG. | TD |
|---|---|---|---|---|---|
| **DET:** Jones | 12 | 44 | 3.7 | 29 | 0 |
| Bryson | 1 | 1 | 1.0 | 1 | 0 |
| Kitna | 1 | 1 | 1.0 | 1 | 1 |
| **CHI:** Jones | 21 | 64 | 3.0 | 15 | 0 |
| Benson | 10 | 25 | 2.5 | 6 | 0 |
| Peterson | 1 | 1 | 1.0 | 1 | 0 |
| Grossman | 1 | 0 | 0.0 | 0 | 0 |
| Griese | 1 | -1 | -1.0 | -1 | 0 |

| RECEIVING | NO. | YDS. | AVG. | LNG. | TD |
|---|---|---|---|---|---|
| **DET:** R. Williams | 6 | 71 | 11.8 | 23 | 0 |
| Furrey | 6 | 67 | 11.2 | 17 | 0 |
| Jones | 6 | 38 | 6.3 | 16 | 0 |
| Pollard | 2 | 19 | 9.5 | 10 | 0 |
| Campbell | 1 | 23 | 23.0 | 23 | 0 |
| Drummond | 1 | 8 | 8.0 | 8 | 0 |
| Bryson | 1 | 4 | 4.0 | 4 | 0 |
| **CHI:** Berrian | 5 | 89 | 17.8 | 41 | 1 |
| Clark | 5 | 85 | 17.0 | 31 | 1 |
| Muhammad | 4 | 59 | 14.8 | 20 | 0 |
| McKie | 2 | 15 | 7.5 | 8 | 0 |
| Gilmore | 2 | 8 | 4.0 | 5 | 2 |
| Davis | 1 | 31 | 31.0 | 31 | 0 |
| Bradley | 1 | 5 | 5.0 | 5 | 0 |
| Jones | 1 | 2 | 2.0 | 2 | 0 |

**INTERCEPTIONS** (NO.-RETURN YARDS)
None

**FUMBLES LOST**
**DET:** Jones 2, Kitna  **CHI:** Berrian

**TIME:** 2:55 • **PAID ATTENDANCE:** 62,181

---

## GAME 3 • SEPT. 24 AT METRODOME

| | | | | | |
|---|---|---|---|---|---|
| **BEARS** | 3 | 0 | 6 | 10 | **19** |
| **VIKINGS** | 3 | 3 | 0 | 10 | **16** |

### SCORING
**FIRST QUARTER**
**VIKINGS:** Longwell 31 FG, 10:49
**BEARS:** Gould 41 FG, 6:20

**SECOND QUARTER**
**VIKINGS:** Longwell 26 FG, 1:08

**THIRD QUARTER**
**BEARS:** Gould 24 FG, 10:53
**BEARS:** Gould 31 FG, 3:18

**FOURTH QUARTER**
**VIKINGS:** Winfield 7 interception return (Longwell kick), 14:53
**BEARS:** Gould 49 FG, 10:37
**VIKINGS:** Longwell 41 FG, 7:27
**BEARS:** Davis 24 pass from Grossman (Gould kick), 1:53

### TEAM STATS

| CATEGORY | CHI | MINN |
|---|---|---|
| First downs | 19 | 11 |
| (Rush-pass-penalty) | 3-14-2 | 3-7-1 |
| Third downs | 5-15 | 5-15 |
| Fourth downs | 1-1 | 0-1 |
| Total net yards | 325 | 286 |
| Rushes-yards | 21-51 | 24-97 |
| Passing yards | 274 | 189 |
| Att.-comp.-int. | 41-23-2 | 31-21-0 |
| Sacked-yards lost | 1-4 | 1-5 |
| Kick returns-yards | 5-129 | 6-119 |
| Punt returns-yards | 3-12 | 2-16 |
| Punts-average | 3-50.7 | 4-39.8 |
| Fumbles-lost | 0-0 | 2-2 |
| Penalties-yards | 10-82 | 8-83 |
| Possession | 28:21 | 31:39 |

### INDIVIDUAL LEADERS

| PASSING | ATT. | COMP. | YDS. | TD | INT. |
|---|---|---|---|---|---|
| **CHI:** Grossman | 41 | 23 | 278 | 1 | 2 |
| **MINN:** Johnson | 31 | 21 | 194 | 0 | 0 |

| RUSHING | NO. | YDS. | AVG. | LNG. | TD |
|---|---|---|---|---|---|
| **CHI:** Jones | 18 | 54 | 3.0 | 17 | 0 |
| Grossman | 3 | -3 | -1.0 | -1 | 0 |
| **MINN:** C. Taylor | 20 | 74 | 3.7 | 24 | 0 |
| Moore | 3 | 23 | 7.7 | 10 | 0 |
| Johnson | 1 | 0 | 0.0 | 0 | 0 |

| RECEIVING | NO. | YDS. | AVG. | LNG. | TD |
|---|---|---|---|---|---|
| **CHI:** Muhammad | 9 | 118 | 13.1 | 24 | 0 |
| Berrian | 6 | 70 | 11.7 | 21 | 0 |
| Davis | 3 | 48 | 16.0 | 24 | 1 |
| Jones | 3 | 11 | 3.7 | 8 | 0 |
| Clark | 2 | 31 | 15.5 | 17 | 0 |
| **MINN:** T. Taylor | 6 | 82 | 13.7 | 36 | 0 |
| Williamson | 4 | 39 | 9.8 | 19 | 0 |
| Moore | 3 | 18 | 6.0 | 10 | 0 |
| C. Taylor | 3 | 15 | 5.0 | 5 | 0 |
| McMullen | 2 | 21 | 10.5 | 20 | 0 |
| Wiggins | 1 | 9 | 9.0 | 9 | 0 |
| Richardson | 1 | 7 | 7.0 | 7 | 0 |
| Kleinsasser | 1 | 3 | 3.0 | 3 | 0 |

**INTERCEPTIONS** (NO.-RETURN YARDS)
**MINN:** Smith (1-30), Winfield (1-7)

**FUMBLES LOST**
**MINN:** Johnson, T. Taylor

**TIME:** 3:10 • **PAID ATTENDANCE:** 63,754

---

## GAME 4 • OCT. 1 AT SOLDIER FIELD

| | | | | | |
|---|---|---|---|---|---|
| **SEAHAWKS** | 3 | 3 | 0 | 0 | **6** |
| **BEARS** | 7 | 13 | 14 | 3 | **37** |

### SCORING
**FIRST QUARTER**
**SEAHAWKS:** Brown 23 FG, 8:58
**BEARS:** Muhammad 9 pass from Grossman (Gould kick), 2:27

**SECOND QUARTER**
**BEARS:** Gould 36 FG, 13:33
**BEARS:** Gould 20 FG, 6:23
**BEARS:** Jones 3 run (Gould kick), 2:25
**SEAHAWKS:** Brown 24 FG, 0:27

**THIRD QUARTER**
**BEARS:** Jones 1 run (Gould kick), 10:05
**BEARS:** Berrian 40 pass from Grossman (Gould kick), 0:51

**FOURTH QUARTER**
**BEARS:** Gould 41 FG, 7:43

### TEAM STATS

| CATEGORY | SEA | CHI |
|---|---|---|
| First downs | 14 | 21 |
| (Rush-pass-penalty) | 4-9-1 | 11-9-1 |
| Third downs | 4-16 | 6-15 |
| Fourth downs | 0-0 | 1-1 |
| Total net yards | 230 | 362 |
| Rushes-yards | 19-77 | 38-143 |
| Passing yards | 153 | 219 |
| Att.-comp.-int. | 37-17-2 | 31-17-0 |
| Sacked-yards lost | 5-49 | 1-13 |
| Kick returns-yards | 7-167 | 3-77 |
| Punt returns-yards | 2-6 | 5-45 |
| Punts-average | 8-43.1 | 5-42.2 |
| Fumbles-lost | 0-0 | 3-0 |
| Penalties-yards | 7-59 | 5-60 |
| Possession | 24:28 | 35:32 |

### INDIVIDUAL LEADERS

| PASSING | ATT. | COMP. | YDS. | TD | INT. |
|---|---|---|---|---|---|
| **SEA:** Hasselbeck | 35 | 16 | 196 | 0 | 2 |
| Wallace | 2 | 1 | 6 | 0 | 0 |
| **CHI:** Grossman | 31 | 17 | 232 | 2 | 0 |

| RUSHING | NO. | YDS. | AVG. | LNG. | TD |
|---|---|---|---|---|---|
| **SEA:** Morris | 11 | 35 | 3.2 | 15 | 0 |
| Hasselbeck | 1 | 19 | 19.0 | 19 | 0 |
| Strong | 4 | 15 | 3.8 | 5 | 0 |
| Weeks | 3 | 8 | 2.7 | 3 | 0 |
| **CHI:** Jones | 24 | 98 | 4.1 | 29 | 2 |
| Benson | 11 | 37 | 3.4 | 19 | 0 |
| Berrian | 1 | 5 | 5.0 | 5 | 0 |
| Grossman | 2 | 2 | 2.0 | 2 | 0 |
| McKie | 1 | 1 | 1.0 | 1 | 0 |

| RECEIVING | NO. | YDS. | AVG. | LNG. | TD |
|---|---|---|---|---|---|
| **SEA:** Jackson | 5 | 62 | 12.4 | 22 | 0 |
| Engram | 4 | 33 | 8.3 | 12 | 0 |
| Branch | 3 | 57 | 19.0 | 31 | 0 |
| Strong | 2 | 14 | 7.0 | 8 | 0 |
| Burleson | 1 | 19 | 19.0 | 19 | 0 |
| Mili | 1 | 15 | 15.0 | 15 | 0 |
| Morris | 1 | 2 | 2.0 | 2 | 0 |
| **CHI:** Muhammad | 5 | 45 | 9.0 | 14 | 1 |
| Berrian | 3 | 108 | 36.0 | 46 | 1 |
| Clark | 3 | 39 | 13.0 | 17 | 0 |
| McKie | 3 | 12 | 4.0 | 9 | 0 |
| Jones | 2 | 9 | 4.5 | 8 | 0 |
| Reid | 1 | 19 | 19.0 | 19 | 0 |

**INTERCEPTIONS** (NO.-RETURN YARDS)
**CHI:** R. Manning (2-52)

**FUMBLES LOST**
None

**TIME:** 3:00 • **PAID ATTENDANCE:** 62,225

## GAME 5 • OCT. 8 AT SOLDIER FIELD

| | | | | | |
|---|---|---|---|---|---|
| **BILLS** | 0 | 0 | 0 | 7 | **7** |
| **BEARS** | 6 | 21 | 3 | 10 | **40** |

### SCORING

**FIRST QUARTER**
**BEARS:** Gould 42 FG, 9:07
**BEARS:** Gould 43 FG, 3:43

**SECOND QUARTER**
**BEARS:** Berrian 8 pass from Grossman (Gould kick), 13:01
**BEARS:** Benson 1 run (Gould kick), 8:30
**BEARS:** Davis 15 pass from Grossman (Gould kick), 4:22

**THIRD QUARTER**
**BEARS:** Gould 32 FG, 7:05

**FOURTH QUARTER**
**BEARS:** Gould 41 FG, 6:05
**BEARS:** Benson 1 run (Gould kick), 4:36
**BILLS:** Evans 5 pass from Losman (Lindell kick), 1:06

### TEAM STATS

| CATEGORY | BUF | CHI |
|---|---|---|
| First downs | 10 | 23 |
| (Rush-pass-penalty) | 3-6-1 | 11-10-2 |
| Third downs | 2-11 | 7-14 |
| Fourth downs | 0-1 | 0-0 |
| Total net yards | 145 | 351 |
| Rushes-yards | 18-58 | 39-155 |
| Passing yards | 87 | 196 |
| Att.-comp.-int. | 27-14-3 | 31-19-0 |
| Sacked-yards lost | 3-28 | 2-15 |
| Kick returns-yards | 7-159 | 2-28 |
| Punt returns-yards | 1-15 | 4-42 |
| Punts-average | 6-57.8 | 3-39.7 |
| Fumbles-lost | 3-2 | 1-1 |
| Penalties-yards | 7-44 | 4-21 |
| Possession | 22:29 | 37:31 |

### INDIVIDUAL LEADERS

| PASSING | ATT. | COMP. | YDS. | TD | INT. |
|---|---|---|---|---|---|
| **BUF:** Losman | 27 | 14 | 115 | 1 | 3 |
| **CHI:** Grossman | 27 | 15 | 182 | 2 | 0 |
| Griese | 4 | 4 | 29 | 0 | 0 |

| RUSHING | NO. | YDS. | AVG. | LNG. | TD |
|---|---|---|---|---|---|
| **BUF:** McGahee | 14 | 50 | 3.6 | 11 | 0 |
| Losman | 3 | 8 | 2.7 | 7 | 0 |
| Moorman | 1 | 0 | 0.0 | 0 | 0 |
| **CHI:** Jones | 22 | 109 | 5.0 | 14 | 0 |
| Benson | 14 | 48 | 3.4 | 11 | 2 |
| Griese | 3 | -2 | -0.7 | 0 | 0 |

| RECEIVING | NO. | YDS. | AVG. | LNG. | TD |
|---|---|---|---|---|---|
| **BUF:** Evans | 9 | 94 | 10.4 | 19 | 1 |
| McGahee | 4 | 15 | 3.8 | 12 | 0 |
| Price | 1 | 6 | 6.0 | 6 | 0 |
| **CHI:** Berrian | 4 | 97 | 24.3 | 62 | 1 |
| Jones | 4 | 13 | 3.3 | 7 | 0 |
| Davis | 3 | 41 | 13.7 | 19 | 1 |
| Gage | 2 | 17 | 8.5 | 13 | 0 |
| Benson | 2 | 14 | 7.0 | 9 | 0 |
| Muhammad | 2 | 10 | 5.0 | 5 | 0 |
| Clark | 1 | 12 | 12.0 | 12 | 0 |
| Gilmore | 1 | 7 | 7.0 | 7 | 0 |

**INTERCEPTIONS** (NO.-RETURN YARDS)
**CHI:** Briggs (1-18), A. Brown (1-18), R. Manning (1-7)

**FUMBLES LOST**
**BUF:** McGee, Moorman  **CHI:** Griese

**TIME:** 2:55 • **PAID ATTENDANCE:** 62,206

---

## GAME 6 • OCT. 16 AT UNIV. OF PHOENIX STADIUM

| | | | | | |
|---|---|---|---|---|---|
| **BEARS** | 0 | 0 | 10 | 14 | **24** |
| **CARDINALS** | 14 | 6 | 3 | 0 | **23** |

### SCORING

**FIRST QUARTER**
**CARDINALS:** Johnson 11 pass from Leinart (Rackers kick), 7:06
**CARDINALS:** Boldin 26 pass from Leinart (Rackers kick), 0:54

**SECOND QUARTER**
**CARDINALS:** Rackers 41 FG, 4:15
**CARDINALS:** Rackers 28 FG, 0:00

**THIRD QUARTER**
**BEARS:** Gould 23 FG, 7:22
**CARDINALS:** Rackers 29 FG, 1:47
**BEARS:** M. Brown 3 fumble return (Gould kick), 0:02

**FOURTH QUARTER**
**BEARS:** Tillman 40 fumble return (Gould kick), 5:00
**BEARS:** Hester 83 punt return (Gould kick), 2:58

### TEAM STATS

| CATEGORY | CHI | ARIZ |
|---|---|---|
| First downs | 9 | 17 |
| (Rush-pass-penalty) | 2-7-0 | 4-12-1 |
| Third downs | 4-14 | 6-20 |
| Fourth downs | 0-1 | 0-0 |
| Total net yards | 168 | 286 |
| Rushes-yards | 16-34 | 38-66 |
| Passing yards | 134 | 220 |
| Att.-comp.-int. | 37-14-4 | 42-24-0 |
| Sacked-yards lost | 2-14 | 1-12 |
| Kick returns-yards | 5-106 | 4-105 |
| Punt returns-yards | 6-152 | 4-42 |
| Punts-average | 6-49.8 | 8-47.4 |
| Fumbles-lost | 2-2 | 2-2 |
| Penalties-yards | 6-50 | 9-65 |
| Possession | 20:17 | 39:43 |

### INDIVIDUAL LEADERS

| PASSING | ATT. | COMP. | YDS. | TD | INT. |
|---|---|---|---|---|---|
| **CHI:** Grossman | 37 | 14 | 148 | 0 | 4 |
| **ARIZ:** Leinart | 42 | 24 | 232 | 2 | 0 |

| RUSHING | NO. | YDS. | AVG. | LNG. | TD |
|---|---|---|---|---|---|
| **CHI:** Jones | 11 | 43 | 3.9 | 11 | 0 |
| Benson | 1 | 4 | 4.0 | 4 | 0 |
| McKie | 1 | -2 | -2.0 | -2 | 0 |
| Grossman | 3 | -7 | -2.3 | -1 | 0 |
| **ARIZ:** James | 36 | 55 | 1.5 | 12 | 0 |
| Arrington | 2 | 11 | 5.5 | 6 | 0 |

| RECEIVING | NO. | YDS. | AVG. | LNG. | TD |
|---|---|---|---|---|---|
| **CHI:** Clark | 4 | 61 | 15.3 | 26 | 0 |
| Jones | 3 | 14 | 4.7 | 6 | 0 |
| Davis | 2 | 31 | 15.5 | 16 | 0 |
| Berrian | 2 | 31 | 15.5 | 17 | 0 |
| Benson | 1 | 8 | 8.0 | 8 | 0 |
| Muhammad | 1 | 2 | 2.0 | 2 | 0 |
| McKie | 1 | 1 | 1.0 | 1 | 0 |
| **ARIZ:** Boldin | 12 | 136 | 11.3 | 26 | 1 |
| Walters | 4 | 25 | 6.3 | 8 | 0 |
| Arrington | 2 | 22 | 11.0 | 12 | 0 |
| Johnson | 2 | 17 | 8.5 | 11 | 1 |
| Ayanbadejo | 2 | 16 | 8.0 | 13 | 0 |
| Pope | 1 | 9 | 9.0 | 9 | 0 |
| James | 1 | 7 | 7.0 | 7 | 0 |

**INTERCEPTIONS** (NO.-RETURN YARDS)
**ARIZ:** Francisco (1-44), Hayes (1-24), Griffith (1-7), Dockett (1- -1)

**FUMBLES LOST**
**CHI:** Grossman 2  **ARIZ:** James, Leinart

**TIME:** 3:23 • **PAID ATTENDANCE:** 63,977

---

## GAME 7 • OCT. 29 AT SOLDIER FIELD

| | | | | | |
|---|---|---|---|---|---|
| **49ERS** | 0 | 0 | 0 | 10 | **10** |
| **BEARS** | 24 | 17 | 0 | 0 | **41** |

### SCORING

**FIRST QUARTER**
**BEARS:** Gould 43 FG, 12:05
**BEARS:** Jones 7 run (Gould kick), 10:39
**BEARS:** Muhammad 5 pass from Grossman (Gould kick), 1:55
**BEARS:** Benson 1 run (Gould kick), 1:02

**SECOND QUARTER**
**BEARS:** Clark 1 pass from Grossman (Gould kick), 10:33
**BEARS:** Gould 36 FG, 3:15
**BEARS:** Clark 27 pass from Grossman (Gould kick), 0:10

**FOURTH QUARTER**
**49ERS:** Nedney 23 FG, 11:35
**49ERS:** Bryant 16 pass from Smith (Nedney kick), 6:49

### TEAM STATS

| CATEGORY | SF | CHI |
|---|---|---|
| First downs | 12 | 24 |
| (Rush-pass-penalty) | 5-6-1 | 7-15-2 |
| Third downs | 3-10 | 7-14 |
| Fourth downs | 0-1 | 1-2 |
| Total net yards | 262 | 402 |
| Rushes-yards | 18-130 | 35-145 |
| Passing yards | 132 | 257 |
| Att.-comp.-int. | 26-16-1 | 32-25-0 |
| Sacked-yards lost | 2-14 | 1-6 |
| Kick returns-yards | 6-126 | 3-73 |
| Punt returns-yards | 2-31 | 1-42 |
| Punts-average | 4-39.0 | 3-51.3 |
| Fumbles-lost | 5-4 | 2-0 |
| Penalties-yards | 5-38 | 5-49 |
| Possession | 22:55 | 37:05 |

### INDIVIDUAL LEADERS

| PASSING | ATT. | COMP. | YDS. | TD | INT. |
|---|---|---|---|---|---|
| **SF:** Smith | 26 | 16 | 146 | 1 | 1 |
| **CHI:** Grossman | 29 | 23 | 252 | 3 | 0 |
| Griese | 3 | 2 | 11 | 0 | 0 |

| RUSHING | NO. | YDS. | AVG. | LNG. | TD |
|---|---|---|---|---|---|
| **SF:** Gore | 12 | 111 | 9.3 | 53 | 0 |
| Smith | 5 | 23 | 4.6 | 9 | 0 |
| Robinson | 1 | -4 | -4.0 | -4 | 0 |
| **CHI:** Jones | 23 | 111 | 4.8 | 12 | 1 |
| Benson | 8 | 26 | 3.3 | 11 | 1 |
| Peterson | 1 | 10 | 10.0 | 10 | 0 |
| McKie | 1 | 0 | 0.0 | 0 | 0 |
| Griese | 2 | -2 | -1.0 | -1 | 0 |

| RECEIVING | NO. | YDS. | AVG. | LNG. | TD |
|---|---|---|---|---|---|
| **SF:** Bryant | 5 | 58 | 11.6 | 16 | 1 |
| Battle | 4 | 32 | 8.0 | 19 | 0 |
| Johnson | 3 | 40 | 13.3 | 25 | 0 |
| Gore | 2 | 9 | 4.5 | 6 | 0 |
| Robinson | 2 | 7 | 3.5 | 4 | 0 |
| **CHI:** Clark | 6 | 86 | 14.3 | 27 | 2 |
| Muhammad | 5 | 65 | 13.0 | 27 | 1 |
| Berrian | 5 | 41 | 8.2 | 15 | 0 |
| Jones | 4 | 23 | 5.8 | 7 | 0 |
| McKie | 3 | 37 | 12.3 | 26 | 0 |
| Peterson | 1 | 8 | 8.0 | 8 | 0 |
| Benson | 1 | 3 | 3.0 | 3 | 0 |

**INTERCEPTIONS** (NO.-RETURN YARDS)
**CHI:** Urlacher (1-0)

**FUMBLES LOST**
**SF:** Smith 2, Bryant, Hicks

**TIME:** 3:56 • **PAID ATTENDANCE:** 62,200

---

## GAME 8 • NOV. 5 AT SOLDIER FIELD

| | | | | | |
|---|---|---|---|---|---|
| **DOLPHINS** | 0 | 14 | 7 | 10 | **31** |
| **BEARS** | 3 | 7 | 3 | 0 | **13** |

### SCORING

**FIRST QUARTER**
**BEARS:** Gould 38 FG, 0:04

**SECOND QUARTER**
**DOLPHINS:** Booker 5 pass from Harrington (Mare kick), 10:47
**DOLPHINS:** Taylor 20 interception return (Mare kick), 10:32
**BEARS:** Muhammad 30 pass from Grossman (Gould kick), 1:57

**THIRD QUARTER**
**DOLPHINS:** Welker 6 pass from Harrington (Mare kick), 13:13
**BEARS:** Gould 38 FG, 1:02

**FOURTH QUARTER**
**DOLPHINS:** Chambers 24 pass from Harrington (Mare kick), 10:00
**DOLPHINS:** Mare 20 FG, 1:09

### TEAM STATS

| CATEGORY | MIA | CHI |
|---|---|---|
| First downs | 17 | 20 |
| (Rush-pass-penalty) | 10-6-1 | 4-10-6 |
| Third downs | 7-17 | 5-16 |
| Fourth downs | 0-0 | 0-2 |
| Total net yards | 298 | 292 |
| Rushes-yards | 35-161 | 28-103 |
| Passing yards | 137 | 189 |
| Att.-comp.-int. | 32-16-2 | 42-18-3 |
| Sacked-yards lost | 0-0 | 3-21 |
| Kick returns-yards | 4-70 | 6-140 |
| Punt returns-yards | 2-13 | 2-11 |
| Punts-average | 6-43.5 | 3-49.0 |
| Fumbles-lost | 0-0 | 4-3 |
| Penalties-yards | 11-69 | 7-45 |
| Possession | 29:54 | 30:06 |

### INDIVIDUAL LEADERS

| PASSING | ATT. | COMP. | YDS. | TD | INT. |
|---|---|---|---|---|---|
| **MIA:** Harrington | 32 | 16 | 137 | 3 | 2 |
| **CHI:** Grossman | 42 | 18 | 210 | 1 | 3 |

| RUSHING | NO. | YDS. | AVG. | LNG. | TD |
|---|---|---|---|---|---|
| **MIA:** Brown | 29 | 157 | 5.4 | 27 | 0 |
| Morris | 1 | 3 | 3.0 | 3 | 0 |
| Harrington | 4 | 2 | 0.5 | 7 | 0 |
| Booker | 1 | -1 | -1.0 | -1 | 0 |
| **CHI:** Jones | 20 | 69 | 3.5 | 11 | 0 |
| Benson | 8 | 34 | 4.3 | 10 | 0 |

| RECEIVING | NO. | YDS. | AVG. | LNG. | TD |
|---|---|---|---|---|---|
| **MIA:** Chambers | 5 | 58 | 11.6 | 24 | 1 |
| Booker | 3 | 14 | 4.7 | 6 | 1 |
| Brown | 2 | 33 | 16.5 | 24 | 0 |
| Welker | 2 | 14 | 7.0 | 8 | 1 |
| McMichael | 1 | 11 | 11.0 | 11 | 0 |
| Hagan | 1 | 7 | 7.0 | 7 | 0 |
| Peelle | 1 | 2 | 2.0 | 2 | 0 |
| Morris | 1 | -2 | -2.0 | -2 | 0 |
| **CHI:** Davis | 5 | 40 | 8.0 | 18 | 0 |
| Jones | 4 | 24 | 6.0 | 9 | 0 |
| Clark | 3 | 38 | 12.7 | 18 | 0 |
| Gage | 2 | 51 | 25.5 | 34 | 0 |
| Muhammad | 2 | 42 | 21.0 | 30 | 1 |
| Berrian | 1 | 10 | 10.0 | 10 | 0 |
| McKie | 1 | 5 | 5.0 | 5 | 0 |

**INTERCEPTIONS** (NO.-RETURN YARDS)
**MIA:** Taylor (1-20), Hill (1-12), Allen (1-7)
**CHI:** A. Brown (1-4), Vasher (1-1)

**FUMBLES LOST**
**CHI:** Gage, Grossman, Hester

**TIME:** 3:23 • **PAID ATTENDANCE:** 62,206

## GAME 9 • NOV. 12 AT THE MEADOWLANDS

| BEARS | 3 | 7 | 14 | 14 | **38** |
|---|---|---|---|---|---|
| GIANTS | 7 | 6 | 7 | 0 | **20** |

### SCORING

**FIRST QUARTER**
GIANTS: Jacobs I run (Feely kick), 9:55
BEARS: Gould 49 FG, 5:59

**SECOND QUARTER**
GIANTS: Feely 46 FG, 13:25
GIANTS: Feely 40 FG, 2:21
BEARS: Bradley 29 pass from Grossman (Gould kick), 0:35

**THIRD QUARTER**
BEARS: Muhammad 10 pass from Grossman (Gould kick), 8:20
BEARS: Clark 2 pass from Grossman (Gould kick), 5:35
GIANTS: Jacobs 8 run (Feely kick), 3:26

**FOURTH QUARTER**
BEARS: Hester 108 FG return (Gould kick), 11:20
BEARS: Jones 2 run (Gould kick), 8:20

### TEAM STATS

| CATEGORY | CHI | NYG |
|---|---|---|
| First downs | 21 | 15 |
| (Rush-pass-penalty) | 7-11-3 | 6-8-1 |
| Third downs | 9-18 | 2-12 |
| Fourth downs | 0-0 | 0-0 |
| Total net yards | 352 | 249 |
| Rushes-yards | 39-118 | 22-150 |
| Passing yards | 234 | 99 |
| Att.-comp.-int. | 30-18-1 | 32-14-2 |
| Sacked-yards lost | 2-12 | 2-22 |
| Kick returns-yards | 5-100 | 7-152 |
| Punt returns-yards | 2-0 | 2-45 |
| Punts-average | 5-39.2 | 5-40.4 |
| Fumbles-lost | 3-2 | 4-1 |
| Penalties-yards | 9-80 | 10-96 |
| Possession | 32:46 | 27:14 |

### INDIVIDUAL LEADERS

| PASSING | ATT. | COMP. | YDS. | TD | INT. |
|---|---|---|---|---|---|
| CHI: Grossman | 30 | 18 | 246 | 3 | 1 |
| NYG: Manning | 32 | 14 | 121 | 0 | 2 |

| RUSHING | NO. | YDS. | AVG. | LNG. | TD |
|---|---|---|---|---|---|
| CHI: Jones | 30 | 113 | 3.8 | 26 | 1 |
| Benson | 6 | 7 | 1.2 | 7 | 0 |
| Grossman | 3 | -2 | -0.7 | 0 | 0 |
| NYG: Barber | 19 | 141 | 7.4 | 46 | 0 |
| Jacobs | 2 | 9 | 4.5 | 8 | 2 |
| Manning | 1 | 0 | 0.0 | 0 | 0 |

| RECEIVING | NO. | YDS. | AVG. | LNG. | TD |
|---|---|---|---|---|---|
| CHI: Muhammmad | 7 | 123 | 17.6 | 25 | 1 |
| Bradley | 4 | 79 | 19.8 | 38 | 1 |
| Jones | 3 | 10 | 3.3 | 8 | 0 |
| Davis | 1 | 26 | 26.0 | 26 | 0 |
| McKie | 1 | 7 | 7.0 | 7 | 0 |
| Clark | 1 | 2 | 2.0 | 2 | 0 |
| Benson | 1 | -1 | -1.0 | -1 | 0 |
| NYG: Burress | 4 | 48 | 12.0 | 16 | 0 |
| Tyree | 4 | 38 | 9.5 | 12 | 0 |
| Barber | 3 | 16 | 5.3 | 7 | 0 |
| Shiancoe | 2 | 4 | 2.0 | 4 | 0 |
| Shockey | 1 | 15 | 15.0 | 15 | 0 |

**INTERCEPTIONS** (NO.-RETURN YARDS)
CHI: Harris (1-16), Tillman (1-11)
NYG: Kiwanuka (1-32)

**FUMBLES LOST**
CHI: Jones, Muhammad  NYG: Manning

**TIME**: 3:22 • **PAID ATTENDANCE**: 78,641

---

## GAME 10 • NOV. 19 AT THE MEADOWLANDS

| BEARS | 0 | 0 | 3 | 7 | **10** |
|---|---|---|---|---|---|
| JETS | 0 | 0 | 0 | 0 | **0** |

### SCORING

**THIRD QUARTER**
BEARS: Gould 20 FG, 10:39

**FOURTH QUARTER**
BEARS: Bradley 57 pass from Grossman (Gould kick), 14:50

### TEAM STATS

| CATEGORY | CHI | NYJ |
|---|---|---|
| First downs | 12 | 15 |
| (Rush-pass-penalty) | 7-4-1 | 5-10-0 |
| Third downs | 4-14 | 6-17 |
| Fourth downs | 1-1 | 1-2 |
| Total net yards | 284 | 265 |
| Rushes-yards | 35-173 | 30-108 |
| Passing yards | 111 | 156 |
| Comp.-att.-int. | 22-11-0 | 35-19-2 |
| Sacked-yards lost | 1-8 | 2-6 |
| Kick returns-yards | 1-0 | 3-48 |
| Punt returns-yards | 1-7 | 2-27 |
| Punts-average | 8-42.9 | 7-44.3 |
| Fumbles-lost | 0-0 | 0-0 |
| Penalties-yards | 10-65 | 6-40 |
| Possession | 28:06 | 31:54 |

### INDIVIDUAL LEADERS

| PASSING | ATT. | COMP. | YDS. | TD | INT. |
|---|---|---|---|---|---|
| CHI: Grossman | 22 | 11 | 119 | 1 | 0 |
| NYJ: Pennington | 35 | 19 | 162 | 0 | 2 |

| RUSHING | NO. | YDS. | AVG. | LNG. | TD |
|---|---|---|---|---|---|
| CHI: Jones | 23 | 121 | 5.3 | 19 | 0 |
| Benson | 10 | 51 | 5.1 | 14 | 0 |
| McKie | 1 | 2 | 2.0 | 2 | 0 |
| Grossman | 1 | -1 | -1.0 | -1 | 0 |
| NYJ: Houston | 11 | 50 | 4.5 | 11 | 0 |
| Dwight | 1 | 28 | 28.0 | 28 | 0 |
| Washington | 13 | 22 | 1.7 | 16 | 0 |
| Smith | 1 | 6 | 6.0 | 6 | 0 |
| Barlow | 4 | 2 | 0.5 | 3 | 0 |

| RECEIVING | NO. | YDS. | AVG. | LNG. | TD |
|---|---|---|---|---|---|
| CHI: Bradley | 4 | 80 | 20.0 | 57 | 1 |
| Muhammad | 2 | 29 | 14.5 | 28 | 0 |
| Jones | 2 | 1 | 0.5 | 3 | 0 |
| Peterson | 1 | 4 | 4.0 | 4 | 0 |
| McKie | 1 | 3 | 3.0 | 3 | 0 |
| Clark | 1 | 2 | 2.0 | 2 | 0 |
| NYJ: Coles | 8 | 80 | 10.0 | 14 | 0 |
| Dwight | 5 | 40 | 8.0 | 15 | 0 |
| Cotchery | 3 | 25 | 8.3 | 22 | 0 |
| Smith | 1 | 7 | 7.0 | 7 | 0 |
| Washington | 1 | 7 | 7.0 | 7 | 0 |
| Baker | 1 | 3 | 3.0 | 3 | 0 |

**INTERCEPTIONS** (NO.-RETURN YARDS)
CHI: Urlacher (1-36), Vasher (1-3)

**FUMBLES LOST**
None

**TIME**: 2:53 • **PAID ATTENDANCE**: 77,632

---

## GAME 11 • NOV. 26 AT GILLETTE STADIUM

| BEARS | 0 | 3 | 0 | 10 | **13** |
|---|---|---|---|---|---|
| PATRIOTS | 0 | 10 | 0 | 7 | **17** |

### SCORING

**SECOND QUARTER**
PATRIOTS: Maroney I run (Gostkowski kick), 9:07
BEARS: Gould 46 FG, 4:04
PATRIOTS: Gostkowski 52 FG, 0:01

**FOURTH QUARTER**
BEARS: Benson 2 run (Gould kick), 14:53
PATRIOTS: Watson 2 pass from Brady (Gostkowski kick), 8:22
BEARS: Gould 32 FG, 3:31

### TEAM STATS

| CATEGORY | CHI | NE |
|---|---|---|
| First downs | 21 | 20 |
| (Rush-pass-penalty) | 9-9-3 | 6-13-1 |
| Third downs | 7-16 | 7-16 |
| Fourth downs | 1-1 | 0-0 |
| Total net yards | 324 | 352 |
| Rushes-yards | 36-153 | 34-85 |
| Passing yards | 171 | 267 |
| Att.-comp.-int. | 34-15-3 | 33-22-2 |
| Sacked-yards lost | 1-5 | 0-0 |
| Kick returns-yards | 3-70 | 4-95 |
| Punt returns-yards | 0-0 | 1-2 |
| Punts-average | 3-38.3 | 3-37.3 |
| Fumbles-lost | 1-1 | 4-3 |
| Penalties-yards | 5-31 | 4-81 |
| Possession | 31:02 | 28:58 |

### INDIVIDUAL LEADERS

| PASSING | ATT. | COMP. | YDS. | TD | INT. |
|---|---|---|---|---|---|
| CHI: Grossman | 34 | 15 | 176 | 0 | 3 |
| NE: Brady | 33 | 22 | 267 | 1 | 2 |

| RUSHING | NO. | YDS. | AVG. | LNG. | TD |
|---|---|---|---|---|---|
| CHI: Jones | 23 | 99 | 4.3 | 17 | 0 |
| Benson | 10 | 46 | 4.6 | 16 | 1 |
| McKie | 1 | 7 | 7.0 | 7 | 0 |
| Grossman | 2 | 1 | 0.5 | 1 | 0 |
| NE: Dillon | 11 | 40 | 3.6 | 26 | 0 |
| Maroney | 13 | 33 | 2.5 | 8 | 1 |
| Brady | 6 | 12 | 2.0 | 11 | 0 |
| Evans | 3 | 8 | 2.7 | 6 | 0 |
| Jackson | 1 | -8 | -8.0 | -8 | 0 |

| RECEIVING | NO. | YDS. | AVG. | LNG. | TD |
|---|---|---|---|---|---|
| CHI: Berrian | 5 | 104 | 20.8 | 47 | 0 |
| Muhammad | 3 | 37 | 12.3 | 18 | 0 |
| Clark | 2 | 14 | 7.0 | 9 | 0 |
| Gilmore | 2 | 5 | 2.5 | 3 | 0 |
| Bradley | 1 | 15 | 15.0 | 15 | 0 |
| Davis | 1 | 3 | 3.0 | 3 | 0 |
| Jones | 1 | -2 | -2.0 | -2 | 0 |
| NE: Watson | 6 | 87 | 14.5 | 40 | 1 |
| Faulk | 6 | 37 | 6.2 | 9 | 0 |
| Maroney | 4 | 45 | 11.3 | 20 | 0 |
| Caldwell | 3 | 57 | 19.0 | 22 | 0 |
| Graham | 1 | 25 | 25.0 | 25 | 0 |
| Brown | 1 | 13 | 13.0 | 13 | 0 |
| Dillon | 1 | 3 | 3.0 | 3 | 0 |

**INTERCEPTIONS** (NO.-RETURN YARDS)
CHI: Tillman (2-8)  NE: Samuel (3-26)

**FUMBLES LOST**
CHI: Grossman  NE: Caldwell, Dillon, Maroney

**TIME**: 3:10 • **PAID ATTENDANCE**: 68,756

---

## GAME 12 • DEC. 3 AT SOLDIER FIELD

| VIKINGS | 0 | 3 | 3 | 7 | **13** |
|---|---|---|---|---|---|
| BEARS | 0 | 7 | 14 | 2 | **23** |

### SCORING

**SECOND QUARTER**
BEARS: Hester 45 punt return (Gould kick), 12:20
VIKINGS: Longwell 23 FG, 8:54

**THIRD QUARTER**
VIKINGS: Longwell 30 FG, 10:07
BEARS: R. Manning 54 interception return (Gould kick), 4:33
BEARS: Benson 24 run (Gould kick), 3:04

**FOURTH QUARTER**
BEARS: Fason tackled in end zone by Ta.Johnson, C.Harris for safety, 13:59
VIKINGS: Fason 4 run (Longwell kick), 5:40

### TEAM STATS

| CATEGORY | MINN | CHI |
|---|---|---|
| First downs | 21 | 6 |
| (Rush-pass-penalty) | 9-8-4 | 5-1-0 |
| Third downs | 4-17 | 2-11 |
| Fourth downs | 1-1 | 1-1 |
| Total net yards | 348 | 107 |
| Rushes-yards | 35-192 | 25-83 |
| Passing yards | 156 | 24 |
| Att.-comp.-int. | 39-21-4 | 19-6-3 |
| Sacked-yards lost | 3-22 | 1-10 |
| Kick returns-yards | 4-62 | 4-85 |
| Punt returns-yards | 3-10 | 3-70 |
| Punts-average | 8-31.1 | 7-43.1 |
| Fumbles-lost | 2-1 | 2-2 |
| Penalties-yards | 12-69 | 9-65 |
| Possession | 39:21 | 20:39 |

### INDIVIDUAL LEADERS

| PASSING | ATT. | COMP. | YDS. | TD | INT. |
|---|---|---|---|---|---|
| MINN: Johnson | 26 | 11 | 73 | 0 | 4 |
| Bollinger | 9 | 7 | 70 | 0 | 0 |
| Jackson | 4 | 3 | 35 | 0 | 0 |
| CHI: Grossman | 19 | 6 | 34 | 0 | 3 |

| RUSHING | NO. | YDS. | AVG. | LNG. | TD |
|---|---|---|---|---|---|
| MINN: C. Taylor | 17 | 99 | 5.8 | 42 | 0 |
| Fason | 11 | 75 | 6.8 | 14 | 1 |
| Moore | 3 | 13 | 4.3 | 6 | 0 |
| Johnson | 3 | 3 | 1.0 | 2 | 0 |
| Jackson | 1 | 2 | 2.0 | 2 | 0 |
| CHI: Benson | 9 | 60 | 6.7 | 24 | 1 |
| Jones | 12 | 32 | 2.7 | 16 | 0 |
| Grossman | 4 | -9 | -2.2 | -2 | 0 |

| RECEIVING | NO. | YDS. | AVG. | LNG. | TD |
|---|---|---|---|---|---|
| MINN: Moore | 5 | 51 | 10.2 | 24 | 0 |
| Robinson | 5 | 37 | 7.4 | 11 | 0 |
| McMullen | 3 | 42 | 14.0 | 19 | 0 |
| Wiggins | 3 | 30 | 10.0 | 24 | 0 |
| T. Taylor | 2 | 9 | 4.5 | 5 | 0 |
| Fason | 2 | 7 | 3.5 | 4 | 0 |
| C. Taylor | 1 | 2 | 2.0 | 2 | 0 |
| CHI: Berrian | 4 | 21 | 5.3 | 10 | 0 |
| McKie | 1 | 8 | 8.0 | 8 | 0 |
| Muhammad | 1 | 5 | 5.0 | 5 | 0 |

**INTERCEPTIONS** (NO.-RETURN YARDS)
CHI: R. Manning (1-54), D. Manning (1-11), Urlacher (1-2), Briggs (1-0)
MINN: Harris (1-11), Winfield (1-0), Leber (1- -10)

**FUMBLES LOST**
MINN: Jackson  CHI: Davis, Wesley

**TIME**: 3:13 • **PAID ATTENDANCE**: 62,221

## GAME 13 • DEC. 11 AT EDWARD JONES DOME

| BEARS | 0 | 14 | 14 | 14 | **42** |
|---|---|---|---|---|---|
| RAMS | 0 | 13 | 0 | 14 | **27** |

### SCORING
**SECOND QUARTER**
**RAMS:** Holt 1 pass from Bulger (kick aborted), 12:45
**BEARS:** Hester 94 kickoff return (Gould kick), 12:32
**RAMS:** Jackson 2 run (Wilkins kick), 7:43
**BEARS:** Berrian 34 pass from Grossman (Gould kick), 3:30
**THIRD QUARTER**
**BEARS:** Jones 30 run (Gould kick), 8:40
**BEARS:** Muhammad 14 pass from Grossman (Gould kick), 3:31
**FOURTH QUARTER**
**BEARS:** Peterson 1 run (Gould kick), 13:04
**RAMS:** Holt 6 pass from Bulger (Wilkins kick), 7:35
**BEARS:** Hester 96 kickoff return (Gould kick), 7:22
**RAMS:** Jackson 6 pass from Bulger (Wilkins kick), 4:41

### TEAM STATS

| CATEGORY | CHI | STL |
|---|---|---|
| First downs | 22 | 28 |
| (Rush-pass-penalty) | 7-10-5 | 5-18-5 |
| Third downs | 6-12 | 6-17 |
| Fourth downs | 0-0 | 3-3 |
| Total net yards | 372 | 473 |
| Rushes-yards | 34-172 | 22-101 |
| Passing yards | 200 | 332 |
| Att.-comp.-int. | 23-13-0 | 55-34-1 |
| Sacked-yards lost | 0-0 | 3-24 |
| Kick returns-yards | 5-228 | 7-150 |
| Punt returns-yards | 1-21 | 1-1 |
| Punts-average | 3-34.7 | 6-45.8 |
| Fumbles-lost | 0-0 | 1-0 |
| Penalties-yards | 11-86 | 11-91 |
| Possession | 26:39 | 33:21 |

### INDIVIDUAL LEADERS

| PASSING | ATT. | COMP. | YDS. | TD | INT. |
|---|---|---|---|---|---|
| CHI: Grossman | 23 | 13 | 200 | 2 | 0 |
| STL: Bulger | 55 | 34 | 356 | 3 | 1 |

| RUSHING | NO. | YDS. | AVG. | LNG. | TD |
|---|---|---|---|---|---|
| CHI: Jones | 11 | 76 | 6.9 | 30 | 1 |
| Benson | 16 | 64 | 4.0 | 9 | 0 |
| Grossman | 3 | 20 | 6.7 | 22 | 0 |
| Peterson | 3 | 12 | 4.0 | 7 | 1 |
| Berrian | 1 | 0 | 0.0 | 0 | 0 |
| STL: Jackson | 18 | 81 | 4.5 | 21 | 1 |
| Davis | 3 | 29 | 9.7 | 16 | 0 |
| Curtis | 1 | -9 | -9.0 | -9 | 0 |

| RECEIVING | NO. | YDS. | AVG. | LNG. | TD |
|---|---|---|---|---|---|
| CHI: Berrian | 3 | 62 | 20.7 | 34 | 1 |
| Muhammmad | 3 | 50 | 16.7 | 21 | 1 |
| Jones | 2 | 26 | 13.0 | 21 | 0 |
| Clark | 2 | 18 | 9.0 | 11 | 0 |
| Peterson | 1 | 32 | 32.0 | 32 | 0 |
| McKie | 1 | 7 | 7.0 | 7 | 0 |
| Davis | 1 | 5 | 5.0 | 5 | 0 |
| STL: Jackson | 10 | 58 | 5.8 | 14 | 1 |
| Holt | 6 | 75 | 12.5 | 26 | 2 |
| Curtis | 4 | 77 | 19.3 | 42 | 0 |
| Bruce | 4 | 62 | 15.5 | 24 | 0 |
| Davis | 4 | 37 | 9.3 | 18 | 0 |
| Klopfenstein | 4 | 31 | 7.8 | 12 | 0 |
| Harris | 1 | 10 | 10.0 | 10 | 0 |
| Walker | 1 | 6 | 6.0 | 6 | 0 |

**INTERCEPTIONS** (NO.-RETURN YARDS)
**CHI:** Tillman (1-0)

**FUMBLES LOST**
None

**TIME:** 3:31 • **PAID ATTENDANCE:** 66,234

---

## GAME 14 • DEC. 17 AT SOLDIER FIELD

| BUCS | 0 | 3 | 7 | 21 | 0 | **31** |
|---|---|---|---|---|---|---|
| BEARS | 7 | 14 | 3 | 7 | 3 | **34** |

### SCORING
**FIRST QUARTER**
**BEARS:** Clark 24 pass from Grossman (Gould kick), 7:42
**SECOND QUARTER**
**BUCS:** Bryant 45 FG, 8:19
**BEARS:** Jones 5 run (Gould kick), 3:58
**BEARS:** Clark 12 pass from Grossman (Gould kick), 0:23
**THIRD QUARTER**
**BEARS:** Gould 38 FG, 5:22
**BUCS:** Alstott 14 run (Bryant kick), 0:25
**FOURTH QUARTER**
**BUCS:** Smith 9 pass from Rattay (Bryant kick), 14:13
**BEARS:** Benson 4 run (Gould kick), 9:23
**BUCS:** Galloway 64 pass from Rattay (Bryant kick), 6:13
**BUCS:** Hilliard 44 pass from Rattay (Bryant kick), 3:44
**OVERTIME**
**BEARS:** Gould 25 FG, 3:37

### TEAM STATS

| CATEGORY | TB | CHI |
|---|---|---|
| First downs | 11 | 27 |
| (Rush-pass-penalty) | 2-8-1 | 7-18-2 |
| Third downs | 6-18 | 5-16 |
| Fourth downs | 0-0 | 0-0 |
| Total net yards | 357 | 446 |
| Rushes-yards | 19-57 | 34-134 |
| Passing yards | 300 | 312 |
| Comp.-att.-int. | 46-25-1 | 44-29-0 |
| Sacked-yards lost | 2-5 | 4-27 |
| Kick returns-yards | 6-117 | 6-85 |
| Punt returns-yards | 7-46 | 7-63 |
| Punts-average | 11-44.5 | 10-44.6 |
| Fumbles-lost | 2-1 | 3-1 |
| Penalties-yards | 9-73 | 8-79 |
| Possession | 29:27 | 41:56 |

### INDIVIDUAL LEADERS

| PASSING | ATT. | COMP. | YDS. | TD | INT. |
|---|---|---|---|---|---|
| TB: Rattay | 35 | 20 | 268 | 3 | 1 |
| Gradkowski | 11 | 5 | 37 | 0 | 0 |
| CHI: Grossman | 44 | 29 | 339 | 2 | 0 |

| RUSHING | NO. | YDS. | AVG. | LNG. | TD |
|---|---|---|---|---|---|
| TB: Williams | 11 | 26 | 2.4 | 7 | 0 |
| Alstott | 6 | 26 | 4.3 | 14 | 1 |
| Pittman | 2 | 5 | 2.5 | 5 | 0 |
| CHI: Jones | 17 | 68 | 4.0 | 8 | 1 |
| Benson | 15 | 53 | 3.5 | 15 | 1 |
| Peterson | 2 | 13 | 6.5 | 11 | 0 |

| RECEIVING | NO. | YDS. | AVG. | LNG. | TD |
|---|---|---|---|---|---|
| TB: Smith | 5 | 24 | 4.8 | 10 | 1 |
| Pittman | 4 | 30 | 7.5 | 14 | 0 |
| Galloway | 3 | 107 | 35.7 | 64 | 1 |
| Hilliard | 3 | 55 | 18.3 | 44 | 1 |
| Stovall | 3 | 42 | 14.0 | 19 | 0 |
| Warren | 2 | 19 | 9.5 | 10 | 0 |
| Williams | 2 | 12 | 6.0 | 7 | 0 |
| Becht | 2 | 12 | 6.0 | 8 | 0 |
| Alstott | 1 | 4 | 4.0 | 4 | 0 |
| CHI: Clark | 7 | 125 | 17.9 | 25 | 2 |
| Muhammad | 6 | 85 | 14.2 | 20 | 0 |
| Berrian | 6 | 33 | 5.5 | 11 | 0 |
| McKie | 5 | 34 | 6.8 | 14 | 0 |
| Jones | 3 | 16 | 5.3 | 9 | 0 |
| Davis | 1 | 28 | 28.0 | 28 | 0 |
| Gilmore | 1 | 18 | 18.0 | 18 | 0 |

**INTERCEPTIONS** (NO.-YARDS)
**CHI:** Harris (1-3)

**FUMBLES LOST**
**TB:** Smith  **CHI:** Hester

**TIME:** 3:48 • **PAID ATTENDANCE:** 62,260

---

## GAME 15 • DEC. 24 AT FORD FIELD

| BEARS | 3 | 14 | 0 | 9 | **26** |
|---|---|---|---|---|---|
| LIONS | 7 | 0 | 14 | 0 | **21** |

### SCORING
**FIRST QUARTER**
**BEARS:** Gould 36 FG, 8:38
**LIONS:** Campbell 23 pass from Kitna (Hanson kick), 2:32
**SECOND QUARTER**
**BEARS:** Berrian 13 pass from Grossman (Gould kick), 14:05
**BEARS:** Peterson 2 run (Gould kick), 0:26
**THIRD QUARTER**
**LIONS:** Furrey 20 pass from Kitna (Hanson kick), 10:53
**LIONS:** Williams 2 pass from Kitna (Hanson kick), 4:27
**FOURTH QUARTER**
**BEARS:** Gould 36 FG, 12:21
**BEARS:** Gould 39 FG, 5:13
**BEARS:** Gould 44 FG, 2:50

### TEAM STATS

| CATEGORY | CHI | DET |
|---|---|---|
| First downs | 22 | 18 |
| (Rush-pass-penalty) | 9-10-3 | 2-15-1 |
| Third downs | 6-17 | 3-13 |
| Fourth downs | 1-1 | 2-3 |
| Total net yards | 354 | 327 |
| Rushes-yards | 30-116 | 18-67 |
| Passing yards | 238 | 260 |
| Att.-comp.-int. | 45-26-0 | 45-27-0 |
| Sacked-yards lost | 2-10 | 3-23 |
| Kick returns-yards | 3-66 | 6-139 |
| Punt returns-yards | 3-18 | 4-61 |
| Punts-average | 6-47.7 | 7-47.9 |
| Fumbles-lost | 0-0 | 2-1 |
| Penalties-yards | 7-48 | 11-92 |
| Possession | 34:43 | 25:17 |

### INDIVIDUAL LEADERS

| PASSING | ATT. | COMP. | YDS. | TD | INT. |
|---|---|---|---|---|---|
| CHI: Grossman | 36 | 20 | 197 | 1 | 0 |
| Griese | 9 | 6 | 51 | 0 | 0 |
| DET: Kitna | 45 | 27 | 283 | 3 | 0 |

| RUSHING | NO. | YDS. | AVG. | LNG. | TD |
|---|---|---|---|---|---|
| CHI: Jones | 12 | 62 | 5.2 | 13 | 0 |
| Benson | 15 | 49 | 3.3 | 10 | 0 |
| Peterson | 3 | 5 | 1.7 | 2 | 1 |
| DET: Harris | 10 | 44 | 4.4 | 18 | 0 |
| Cason | 5 | 31 | 6.2 | 16 | 0 |
| Gordon | 1 | 2 | 2.0 | 2 | 0 |
| Kitna | 1 | -1 | -1.0 | -1 | 0 |
| Ellis | 1 | -9 | -9.0 | -9 | 0 |

| RECEIVING | NO. | YDS. | AVG. | LNG. | TD |
|---|---|---|---|---|---|
| CHI: Berrian | 5 | 43 | 8.6 | 13 | 1 |
| Muhammad | 3 | 64 | 21.3 | 40 | 0 |
| Clark | 3 | 36 | 12.0 | 22 | 0 |
| Bradley | 3 | 28 | 9.3 | 16 | 0 |
| Reid | 3 | 18 | 6.0 | 10 | 0 |
| Jones | 2 | 10 | 5.0 | 11 | 0 |
| Benson | 2 | 8 | 4.0 | 9 | 0 |
| McKie | 2 | 7 | 3.5 | 6 | 0 |
| Peterson | 2 | 7 | 3.5 | 5 | 0 |
| Davis | 1 | 27 | 27.0 | 27 | 0 |
| DET: Furrey | 10 | 107 | 10.7 | 20 | 1 |
| R. Williams | 6 | 79 | 13.2 | 26 | 1 |
| Harris | 5 | 26 | 5.2 | 9 | 0 |
| Campbell | 2 | 31 | 15.5 | 23 | 1 |
| M. Williams | 2 | 22 | 11.0 | 14 | 0 |
| McHugh | 1 | 11 | 11.0 | 11 | 0 |
| Fitzsimmons | 1 | 7 | 7.0 | 7 | 0 |

**INTERCEPTIONS** (NO.-YARDS)
None

**FUMBLES LOST**
**DET:** Kitna

**TIME:** 3:23 • **PAID ATTENDANCE:** 60,665

---

## GAME 16 • DEC. 31 AT SOLDIER FIELD

| PACKERS | 13 | 10 | 0 | 3 | **26** |
|---|---|---|---|---|---|
| BEARS | 0 | 0 | 7 | 0 | **7** |

### SCORING
**FIRST QUARTER**
**PACKERS:** Driver 9 pass from Favre (Rayner kick), 9:31
**PACKERS:** Collins 55 interception return (kick failed), 0:50
**SECOND QUARTER**
**PACKERS:** Rayner 25 FG, 0:49
**PACKERS:** Dendy 30 interception return (Rayner kick), 0:34
**THIRD QUARTER**
**BEARS:** Bradley 75 pass from Griese (Gould kick), 0:34
**FOURTH QUARTER**
**PACKERS:** Rayner 46 FG, 10:39

### TEAM STATS

| CATEGORY | GB | CHI |
|---|---|---|
| First downs | 20 | 13 |
| (Rush-pass-penalty) | 5-14-1 | 6-5-2 |
| Third downs | 11-20 | 2-13 |
| Fourth downs | 0-0 | 1-1 |
| Total net yards | 373 | 316 |
| Rushes-yards | 34-97 | 24-135 |
| Passing yards | 276 | 181 |
| Att.-comp.-int. | 42-21-1 | 28-8-5 |
| Sacked-yards lost | 2-9 | 2-13 |
| Kick returns-yards | 1-26 | 6-129 |
| Punt returns-yards | 3-29 | 3-8 |
| Punts-average | 5-40.0 | 5-41.6 |
| Fumbles-lost | 2-0 | 3-1 |
| Penalties-yards | 3-35 | 6-44 |
| Possession | 36:56 | 23:04 |

### INDIVIDUAL LEADERS

| PASSING | ATT. | COMP. | YDS. | TD | INT. |
|---|---|---|---|---|---|
| GB: Favre | 42 | 21 | 285 | 1 | 1 |
| CHI: Griese | 15 | 5 | 124 | 1 | 2 |
| Grossman | 12 | 2 | 33 | 0 | 3 |
| Maynard | 1 | 1 | 37 | 0 | 0 |

| RUSHING | NO. | YDS. | AVG. | LNG. | TD |
|---|---|---|---|---|---|
| GB: Green | 22 | 71 | 3.2 | 9 | 0 |
| Morency | 9 | 37 | 4.1 | 15 | 0 |
| Martin | 2 | -5 | -2.5 | -2 | 0 |
| Driver | 1 | -6 | -6.0 | -6 | 0 |
| CHI: Benson | 13 | 109 | 8.4 | 30 | 0 |
| Jones | 9 | 27 | 3.0 | 7 | 0 |
| Grossman | 2 | -1 | -0.5 | 0 | 0 |

| RECEIVING | NO. | YDS. | AVG. | LNG. | TD |
|---|---|---|---|---|---|
| GB: Martin | 7 | 118 | 16.9 | 34 | 0 |
| Holiday | 5 | 87 | 17.4 | 35 | 0 |
| Green | 4 | 39 | 9.8 | 16 | 0 |
| Driver | 3 | 23 | 7.7 | 9 | 1 |
| Lee | 1 | 15 | 15.0 | 15 | 0 |
| Henderson | 1 | 3 | 3.0 | 3 | 0 |
| CHI: Davis | 2 | 19 | 9.5 | 13 | 0 |
| Bradley | 1 | 75 | 75.0 | 75 | 1 |
| Peterson | 1 | 37 | 37.0 | 37 | 0 |
| Muhammad | 1 | 27 | 27.0 | 27 | 0 |
| Benson | 1 | 22 | 22.0 | 22 | 0 |
| Berrian | 1 | 17 | 17.0 | 17 | 0 |
| Jones | 1 | -3 | -3.0 | -3 | 0 |

**INTERCEPTIONS** (NO.-RETURN YARDS)
**GB:** Collins (2-63), Dendy (1-30), Hawk (1-6), Woodson (1-3)
**CHI:** Vasher (1-7)

**FUMBLES LOST**
**CHI:** Grossman

**TIME:** 2:54 • **PAID ATTENDANCE:** 62,287

★ NFC SEMIFINAL • JAN. I4 AT SOLDIER FIELD ★

| SEAHAWKS | 0 | 14 | 10 | 0 | 0 | **24** |
| BEARS | 7 | 14 | 0 | 3 | 3 | **27** |

 ★ NFC CHAMPIONSHIP • JAN. 2I AT SOLDIER FIELD ★

| SAINTS | 0 | 7 | 7 | 0 | **14** |
| BEARS | 3 | 13 | 2 | 21 | **39** |

## DRIVES

### FIRST HALF

| | START | PLAYS | YDS. | RESULT |
|---|---|---|---|---|
| CHI | CHI 20 | 12 | 80 | Touchdown |
| SEA | SEA 47 | 3 | 9 | Punt |
| CHI | CHI 7 | 6 | 22 | Punt |
| SEA | SEA 29 | 9 | 71 | Touchdown |
| CHI | CHI 32 | 1 | 68 | Touchdown |
| SEA | SEA 37 | 3 | 3 | Punt |
| CHI | CHI 30 | 4 | 14 | Punt |
| SEA | SEA 24 | 4 | 15 | Punt |
| CHI | CHI 18 | 5 | 17 | Punt |
| SEA | SEA 22 | 3 | 8 | Punt |
| CHI | CHI 42 | 3 | -16 | Fumble |
| SEA | CHI 26 | 5 | 26 | Touchdown |
| CHI | CHI 43 | 7 | 57 | Touchdown |
| SEA | SEA 29 | 2 | 5 | End of Half |

### SECOND HALF

| | START | PLAYS | YDS. | RESULT |
|---|---|---|---|---|
| SEA | SEA 29 | 9 | 49 | Field goal |
| CHI | CHI 31 | 4 | -8 | Punt |
| SEA | SEA 49 | 7 | 51 | Touchdown |
| CHI | CHI 38 | 10 | 52 | Interception |
| SEA | SEA 21 | 1 | 0 | Interception |
| CHI | SEA 32 | 3 | -4 | Punt |
| SEA | SEA 7 | 3 | 3 | Punt |
| CHI | CHI 29 | 12 | 48 | Field goal |
| SEA | SEA 37 | 5 | 17 | Downs |
| CHI | CHI 46 | 3 | 3 | Punt |
| SEA | SEA 20 | 10 | 26 | Downs |

### OVERTIME

| | START | PLAYS | YDS. | RESULT |
|---|---|---|---|---|
| SEA | SEA 30 | 4 | 18 | Punt |
| CHI | CHI 34 | 7 | 34 | Field goal |

## SCORING

### FIRST QUARTER
**BEARS:** Jones 9 run (Gould kick), 8:35

### SECOND QUARTER
**SEAHAWKS:** Burleson 16 pass from Hasselbeck (Brown kick), 14:54
**BEARS:** Berrian 68 pass from Grossman (Gould kick), 14:36
**SEAHAWKS:** Alexander 4 run (Brown kick), 2:29
**BEARS:** Jones 7 run (Gould kick), 0:48

### THIRD QUARTER
**SEAHAWKS:** Brown 40 FG, 9:56
**SEAHAWKS:** Alexander 13 run (Brown kick), 4:57

### FOURTH QUARTER
**BEARS:** Gould 41 FG, 4:24

### OVERTIME
**BEARS:** Gould 49 FG, 10:02

### TEAM STATS

| CATEGORY | SEA | CHI |
|---|---|---|
| First downs | 18 | 21 |
| (Rush-pass-penalty) | 12-6-0 | 8-10-3 |
| Third downs | 5-15 | 8-20 |
| Fourth downs | 1-3 | 1-1 |
| Total net yards | 306 | 371 |
| Rushes-yards | 31-127 | 34-120 |
| Passing yards | 179 | 251 |
| Att.-comp.-int. | 33-18-1 | 38-21-1 |
| Sacked-yards lost | 3-16 | 3-31 |
| Kick returns-yards | 6-166 | 4-73 |
| Punt returns-yards | 3-2 | 3-5 |
| Punts-average | 6-36.3 | 6-40.3 |
| Fumbles-lost | 0-0 | 4-1 |
| Penalties-yards | 4-16 | 5-40 |
| Possession | 29:25 | 35:33 |

## DRIVES

### FIRST HALF

| | START | PLAYS | YDS. | RESULT |
|---|---|---|---|---|
| NO | NO 20 | 5 | 44 | Punt |
| CHI | CHI 20 | 3 | 5 | Punt |
| NO | NO 39 | 5 | -5 | Punt |
| CHI | CHI 40 | 3 | 1 | Punt |
| NO | NO 28 | 4 | 22 | Fumble |
| CHI | NO 36 | 11 | 35 | Field goal |
| NO | — | 0 | 0 | Fumble |
| CHI | NO 30 | 4 | 5 | Field goal |
| NO | NO 24 | 3 | -9 | Punt |
| CHI | NO 49 | 8 | 43 | Field goal |
| NO | NO 20 | 6 | 20 | Punt |
| CHI | CHI 31 | 8 | 69 | Touchdown |
| NO | NO 27 | 8 | 73 | Touchdown |
| CHI | CHI 34 | 3 | 3 | End of half |

### SECOND HALF

| | START | PLAYS | YDS. | RESULT |
|---|---|---|---|---|
| CHI | CHI 24 | 4 | 19 | Punt |
| NO | NO 7 | 2 | 93 | Touchdown |
| CHI | CHI 40 | 3 | -2 | Punt |
| NO | NO 18 | 11 | 53 | Missed FG |
| CHI | CHI 37 | 3 | 7 | Punt |
| NO | NO 5 | 2 | -5 | Safety |
| CHI | NO 36 | 3 | -2 | Punt |
| NO | NO 20 | 4 | 20 | Punt |
| CHI | CHI 15 | 5 | 85 | Touchdown |
| NO | NO 28 | 2 | -2 | Fumble |
| CHI | NO 26 | 4 | 26 | Touchdown |
| NO | NO 26 | 2 | 5 | Interception |
| CHI | CHI 38 | 3 | 8 | Punt |
| NO | NO 8 | 7 | 22 | Downs |
| CHI | NO 30 | 5 | 30 | Touchdown |
| NO | NO 33 | 4 | 9 | Downs |
| CHI | NO 42 | 5 | 8 | End of game |

## SCORING

### FIRST QUARTER
**BEARS:** Gould 19 FG, 0:41

### SECOND QUARTER
**BEARS:** Gould 43 FG, 13:40
**BEARS:** Gould 24 FG, 8:52
**BEARS:** Jones 2 run (Gould kick), 1:56
**SAINTS:** Colston 13 pass from Brees (Carney kick), 0:46

### THIRD QUARTER
**SAINTS:** Bush 88 pass from Brees (Carney kick), 12:20
**BEARS:** Penalty on Brees enforced in end zone for safety, 5:27

### FOURTH QUARTER
**BEARS:** Berrian 33 pass from Grossman (Gould kick), 14:23
**BEARS:** Benson 12 run (Gould kick), 11:37
**BEARS:** Jones 15 run (Gould kick), 4:19

### TEAM STATS

| CATEGORY | NO | CHI |
|---|---|---|
| First downs | 15 | 18 |
| (Rush-pass-penalty) | 3-12-0 | 12-6-0 |
| Third downs | 5-13 | 3-16 |
| Fourth downs | 0-2 | 2-2 |
| Total net yards | 375 | 340 |
| Rushes-yards | 12-56 | 46-196 |
| Passing yards | 319 | 144 |
| Att.-comp.-int. | 49-27-1 | 26-11-0 |
| Sacked-yards lost | 3-35 | 0-0 |
| Kick returns-yards | 7-132 | 3-39 |
| Punt returns-yards | 4-15 | 2-24 |
| Punts-average | 5-38.8 | 7-47.4 |
| Fumbles-lost | 4-3 | 1-0 |
| Penalties-yards | 7-47 | 1-5 |
| Possession | 24:45 | 35:15 |

## INDIVIDUAL STATS

### PASSING

| SEAHAWKS | ATT. | COMP. | YDS. | TD | INT. | BEARS | ATT. | COMP. | YDS. | TD | INT. |
|---|---|---|---|---|---|---|---|---|---|---|---|
| Hasselbeck | 33 | 18 | 195 | 1 | 1 | Grossman | 38 | 21 | 282 | 1 | 1 |

### RUSHING

| SEAHAWKS | NO. | YDS. | AVG. | LNG. | TD | BEARS | NO. | YDS. | AVG. | LNG. | TD |
|---|---|---|---|---|---|---|---|---|---|---|---|
| Alexander | 26 | 108 | 4.2 | 13 | 2 | Jones | 21 | 66 | 3.1 | 9 | 2 |
| Morris | 4 | 11 | 2.8 | 6 | 0 | Benson | 12 | 45 | 3.8 | 12 | 0 |
| Hasselbeck | 1 | 8 | 8.0 | 8 | 0 | Davis | 1 | 9 | 9.0 | 9 | 0 |

### RECEIVING

| SEAHAWKS | NO. | YDS. | AVG. | LNG. | TD | BEARS | NO. | YDS. | AVG. | LNG. | TD |
|---|---|---|---|---|---|---|---|---|---|---|---|
| Jackson | 4 | 49 | 12.3 | 24 | 0 | Berrian | 5 | 105 | 21.0 | 68 | 1 |
| Branch | 4 | 48 | 12.0 | 22 | 0 | Davis | 4 | 84 | 21.0 | 37 | 0 |
| Engram | 3 | 32 | 10.7 | 16 | 0 | Muhammad | 3 | 38 | 12.7 | 21 | 0 |
| Heller | 3 | 20 | 6.7 | 10 | 0 | Benson | 3 | 24 | 8.0 | 11 | 0 |
| Stevens | 2 | 18 | 9.0 | 10 | 0 | Jones | 2 | 6 | 3.0 | 3 | 0 |
| Burleson | 1 | 16 | 16.0 | 16 | 1 | Clark | 1 | 13 | 13.0 | 13 | 0 |
| Alexander | 1 | 12 | 12.0 | 12 | 0 | Bradley | 1 | 5 | 5.0 | 5 | 0 |
| | | | | | | Reid | 1 | 5 | 5.0 | 5 | 0 |
| | | | | | | McKie | 1 | 2 | 2.0 | 2 | 0 |

### INTERCEPTIONS (NO.-RETURN YARDS)
**SEAHAWKS:** Hunter (1-16)    **BEARS:** R. Manning (1-6)

### FUMBLES LOST
**SEAHAWKS:** None    **BEARS:** Grossman

**TIME:** 3:16 • **PAID ATTENDANCE:** 62,184

## INDIVIDUAL STATS

### PASSING

| SAINTS | ATT. | COMP. | YDS. | TD | INT. | BEARS | ATT. | COMP. | YDS. | TD | INT. |
|---|---|---|---|---|---|---|---|---|---|---|---|
| Brees | 49 | 27 | 354 | 2 | 1 | Grossman | 26 | 11 | 144 | 1 | 0 |

### RUSHING

| SAINTS | NO. | YDS. | AVG. | LNG. | TD | BEARS | NO. | YDS. | AVG. | LNG. | TD |
|---|---|---|---|---|---|---|---|---|---|---|---|
| Bush | 4 | 19 | 4.8 | 12 | 0 | Jones | 19 | 123 | 6.5 | 33 | 2 |
| McAllister | 6 | 18 | 3.0 | 6 | 0 | Benson | 24 | 60 | 2.5 | 12 | 1 |
| Karney | 1 | 11 | 11.0 | 11 | 0 | Davis | 1 | 16 | 16.0 | 16 | 0 |
| Brees | 1 | 8 | 8.0 | 8 | 0 | Grossman | 2 | -3 | -1.5 | -1 | 0 |

### RECEIVING

| SAINTS | NO. | YDS. | AVG. | LNG. | TD | BEARS | NO. | YDS. | AVG. | LNG. | TD |
|---|---|---|---|---|---|---|---|---|---|---|---|
| Bush | 7 | 132 | 18.9 | 88 | 1 | Berrian | 5 | 85 | 17.0 | 33 | 1 |
| Colston | 5 | 63 | 12.6 | 29 | 1 | McKie | 3 | 6 | 2.0 | 4 | 0 |
| Miller | 4 | 31 | 7.8 | 12 | 0 | Clark | 1 | 30 | 30.0 | 30 | 0 |
| Copper | 3 | 29 | 9.7 | 14 | 0 | Muhammad | 1 | 20 | 20.0 | 20 | 0 |
| McAllister | 3 | 27 | 9.0 | 15 | 0 | Gilmore | 1 | 3 | 3.0 | 3 | 0 |
| Henderson | 2 | 57 | 28.5 | 40 | 0 | | | | | | |
| Campbell | 2 | 6 | 3.0 | 5 | 0 | | | | | | |
| Karney | 1 | 9 | 9.0 | 9 | 0 | | | | | | |

### INTERCEPTIONS (NO.-RETURN YARDS)
**SAINTS:** None    **BEARS:** Vasher (1-0)

### FUMBLES LOST
**SAINTS:** Brees, Colston, Lewis    **BEARS:** None

**TIME:** 3:10 • **PAID ATTENDANCE:** 61,187

**THANKS, TANK:** Fans slap hands with defensive tackle Tank Johnson after the Bears won the **NFC** championship game. SCOTT STRAZZANTE

**HOT STUFF:** Bears fans Jim Provenzale (left), Kent Ebersold and Mark Baresel warm their hands while tailgating at Adler Planetarium before the **NFC** title game. CHUCK BERMAN

**TRUE BLUE (AND ORANGE):** In more than full Bears regalia, a fan watches the comeback victory at Arizona. JOHN SMIERCIAK

**INGEBURG NECKERMAN of Chicago**

**RYNE HABERKORN of Watseka**

# BEARS FANS PORTRAITS
## Photo essay by MICHAEL TERCHA

SOME BEARS FANS love the team—and others LOVE the team. I went to Soldier Field before the NFC championship game against the Saints to find the latter. Accompanied by an anxious assistant and armed with a 4-foot roll of gray paper for a background and a bag full of lights, I braved the tailgaters' sausage smoke and beer breath to hunt my prey—The "Ultrafan." I set up the portable studio in a secluded spot of the South Parking Lot's covered first floor and began to lure the Ultrafans to my lights. During the morning, I captured the smoking fan, the furry fan, the rock-star fan and the ever-elusive "blue-chested fan," to name a few. All of them were proud of their team, and all of them wore their hearts on their sleeves—or their heads, or their torsos.

**JULIAN WINTERS of Chicago**

**MATTHEW TUCCI, TONY TUCCI AND MARK TUCCI of Gurnee**

**OSCAR BLOMGREN** of Green Oaks

**RICK WEBBER** of Joliet

**DINO-SORE:** Even the brachiosaurus at the Field Museum is a fan of Brian Urlacher's bone-crushing hits. PHIL VELASQUEZ